THE LAST OF
THE GREAT
ROAD RACES

The Isle of Man TT

'You must understand, it really is the last great road race'.

T.T. veteran

SBN 85184-012-4

Published by Transport Bookman Limited
Syon Park, Brentford, London, England

All photographs supplied by the author

Designed and typeset by
Barbara Harris

Cover design by
David Harris

IBM Baskerville 11 on 13

Printed in England by
HGA Printing Company Limited, Brentford, London

Index

The events and races in this book, unless otherwise stated, took place in the 1974 Isle of Man T.T.

Acknowledgements

My sincere thanks to:

Auto Cycle Union, in particular, Vernon Cooper, Ken Shierson, Mary Driver and Brenda Davies.

All the Participants and in particular, Mick Grant, Billie McCosh, Jack Findaly, Paul Smart, Fred and Lesley Lewin, Joe and Alma Rocheleau, Alan Sansum, Mick Jones and Dave Saunders, John Williams, Charlie Williams, Peter Williams.

Keith Callow and Ray Cunningham of Shellsport.

Geoffrey Duke, O.B.E.

Allen Harbinson of Paul Raymond Publications.

The Isle of Man Tourist Board for contributing towards my stay on the Island.

Mrs Talavera of the Marine Hotel, Queens Promenade, Douglas, for coping with my eccentric eating hours.

Mr Collins of the Empress Hotel, Queens Promenade, Douglas, for coping with my eccentric eating hours.

Neil Kelly, Manx motorcycle dealer for a miracle, a motorcycle.

Mylchreests Motor for another miracle — a car.

Peter Knealc of Manx Radio.

Norman Scott of the T.T. Veterans Association and all the grand men who told me about the way it was.

Vince Davey, Manager, Gus Kuhn Motorcycles for initiating me into the mysteries.

Brands Hatch for generously allowing me entry at various times.

Pete Kelly and staff of Motor Cycle.

Peter Strong and staff of Motor Cycle News.

Finally to all those television companies, without whose polite indifference this book would never have been written.

Embarking in the luxury of Liverpool

Chapter 1

'I hate it, I wouldn't go there no matter what they paid me.'
Barry Sheene

It was the second day of practice for the Isle of Man T.T. races, and I had walked into the enclosure where the motorcycles and side cars were being variously polished, warmed up, listened to or determinedly ignored. This enclosure was oddly known as the paddock. The horses of the technological age gleamed in the afternoon sun and far below the sea answered with metallic fire. Down a row of motorcycles I went, absorbing everything, the sights and the smells. Here I felt it for the first time, an odd, shared group tension. It seemed somehow natural even in the gentle afternoon's warmth, for was this not a week's prelude to the most demanding race of them all — the Tourist Trophy.

That air of tension was most palpable in a couple I noticed. He was young and slim in his black racing leathers and she was undeniably beautiful. They lay on the grass next to his motorcycle, holding and kissing one another as though he was leaving for a war in a foreign land.

An older man, his belly just protruding through his tight leathers, walked by, then stopped. He looked at the two young lovers holding one another so terribly, their eyes closed.

'Ere now lad,' he said in a broad Lancastrian accent, 'tha's not at Blackpool now — give over.'

They held each other for another moment then the rider slowly got up, pulled on his gloves and a crash helmet and pushed his bike into screaming life. His woman followed him to the starting grid. A light winked and he was away. She clicked a stop watch.

Chapter 1

'Do you get nervous for him?'
She looked at me quickly as though to avert accident by ignoring me.
'Do you...'
'Yes very.'
And she walked away blushing at her treachery. I noted his number, 56, Steve Galpin, riding in the Ultra Lightweight Class. The smallest and slowest of all the motorcycles. How did the men racing the big ones and their women feel?

Up on the Grandstand I climbed to the highest seats where I was alone and could observe the activity going on below. Every now and again the air would be torn apart by the high pitched screams of the Japanese two-strokes as they split the air on the home straight. There was a smell of 'Castrol R' oil in the air, a comfortable pungency taking me back to my youth, dimly lit garages and Matchboxes and Velos and Aye Jays and all the names of bikes that were once great and are now dead.

Because I am a creature of habit and had not yet had time to read the morning paper I unfolded it and started on the front page. Down below, the sidecar combinations were warming up. Their engines, slower revving four-strokes, gave out a solid more comforting roar, than the jarring crackle of the solo motorcycles. Then in the midst of the noise, the smells and the ceaseless activity going on down below me, I saw it. A small insert at the foot of the page.

> Mr Peter Hardy was killed yesterday in practice on
> his sidecar on the Isle of Man . . . .

In that split second of identification my world went dead quiet. How did he die? What was he doing? In that last terrible moment, before idea and act become extinguished by reality, did he fight the bucking juddering machine, trying by skill and will to dominate death? And when the doomed noises had died down, was his end fast and painless — or did he fight on?

The article mentioned that his passenger, his twin brother, had sustained minor injuries and was on his way home. I grieved for him and it was then, because I knew so little, that I wondered whether these racers were not all suicidal, or at least terribly self-destructive.

I noticed then that the grandstand overlooked not only the home straight but also the cemetery with its orderly tributes to man's frailty. My body, unused to walking, not sleeping, irregular meals, was tired and sore, but I could not stay where I was. To exorcise the dread moment I went down to the paddock again and wandered around the machines, watching the riders, sculpturally beautiful in their leathers, talking to their mechanics, managers, friends and women. I still could not understand why they came here to race. A short while ago at Brands Hatch I had spoken to Barry Sheene, a works Suzuki rider. He was surrounded by a large group of admirers and in the sunshine had stripped off the top of his leathers. Dangling about his waist, they revealed a large surgical dressing, plastered starkly on his suntanned back, a leftover from a recent accident. Looking at him I could understand why the people crowded around him. He was classically attractive in face and body, and an even bigger attraction — this young man was very shortly about to challenge the gods again. They knew it and he knew it. The threat of death was almost a sexual thrill in the air.
'Oh Barry, sign here please.'
A firm breast covered only by a Barry Sheene T-shirt was thrust at him. He lifted his dark glasses showing two incredibly bloodshot eyes, surveyed the area he was about to sign approvingly and then pulling the T-shirt tight, signed with a flourish. The males in the crowd whistled. Sheene looked at the girl carefully and nodded slightly. Someone else thrust a programme at him.
'Here please Barry.'
He signed still looking at the girl. I pushed my way through the crowd, it was obvious there was not going to be a quiet moment for any questions.
'Excuse me, are you going to the Isle of Man T.T.?'

Chapter 1

He looked up at me sharply.

'No.'

'Why?'

'I hate it. I wouldn't go there no matter what they paid me. The race is a death trap. I don't care what anyone says.'

With a look he dared me to challenge his expert opinion. Then I knew something else, he was ashamed that he was not racing there, for in some obscure way the race is still the ultimate test of a rider's skill, courage and hence, manhood.

His mechanic handed him a pair of crutches and he hobbled off to the starting grid. He had a broken foot as well, and yet he was racing here. I left Sheene with his anger and went and spoke to a rider whom I knew was going over to the Island, John Williams. He introduced me to his wife and astounded me with the information that as well as being a top rider, he owned and ran a fashion boutique in Cheshire.

So today in the paddock on the Island, I halloed him again as he was waiting to do one more lap before the solos were called in and the sidecars were set off.

'How do you feel?'

He smiled and nodded.

'Alright.'

It seemed as good a time as any.

'Nervous?'

He looked at me in the strange unblinking way that most fast riders seem to have.

'Yes,' he said, 'a bit.'

'Like yesterday?'

He had won some of the races at Brands, but the event and the track seemed light years away. Very carefully, his jaw muscles moving just perceptibly with the tension, he said,

'When I'm racing, I have to get into the right frame of mind. I have to concentrate, get all the juices right, then I know I'm going to win.'

He jerked his thumb in the direction of the other riders, 'And so
do they.'
'And now?'
'This is practice, but you have to watch it like . . .'
His mechanic said something to him and he left immediately for
his motorcycle. There is a very definite order of priorities when
one is racing and an author is a low man on the totem pole.

I wandered in amongst the other riders remembering Sheene's
comment and contemplating the fact that of the world's top riders
only a few would be here. There were many reasons for this, but
undeniably the strongest, though seldom vouchsafed, was that
circuit races are usually run on two miles of specially prepared and
banked track, while the Isle of Man T.T. races are run over thirty
seven miles of twisting, turning, ordinary, (in some places extra-
ordinarily ordinary) roads. On an unknown circuit it its possible for a
good rider to come in, practise for a day *and expect to win a race*
the next day. On the Isle of Man, the rider has not been born who
can do this. He has to learn the correct line on every corner, he has
to remember not only that corner, but the next and sometimes up
to three. ('If you miss the first you're in dead trouble on the other
three.' — a rider describing a sweep of four linked bends on the
mountain section.) And then when the rider has a precise knowledge
of the bends, kinks and curves of the road, he has to judge to a
nicety how fast he can negotiate them. A misjudgement here will
not necessarily result in a slide into a grass verge or a straw bale.
For on the side of this road, there are garden walls, steep banks,
telegraph poles, trees, bus shelters, gates and even the occasional
animal — though latterly these are few and far between. (Charlie
Williams did however complain later in the week that 'a bloody cat
sat watching me on the corner. I could have touched the bugger if
I wanted — it didn't move as I went round.')

So many of the top European championship names were missing,
most of them because the course is too long, too difficult, too demanding and also, although no one said this, it's a very British race.

Chapter 1

Where else would a crumbling structure of wood and corrugated iron painted a faded green be called a 'Grandstand'? What other race would have each pit stop area too small for the full length of a motorcycle and adorned by quaint yellow containers? These, I was gravely informed, were 'gravity fillers' i.e. they do not pump the petrol in, but let it fall out. Where else would you find the ethos of 'make do and get on with it' so completely embodied? The riders come here at huge personal expense, most scrape by on inadequate meals, poor accomodation and little sleep and what is more, come back year after year.

Vernon Cooper, Chairman of the Auto Cycle Union's Road Racing Committee has been to America and seen how they run the Indianapolis 500.
'We need more hoopla here, bands, drum majorettes and that sort of stuff.'
I can see it now, the Grimethorpe Colliery Brass Band, marching up and down on the promenade with comments from the spectators like 'Bloody 'ell, thought we'd left them buggers behind.' And a bevy of plump Northern beauties, dropping their batons, their flesh bulging out of their satin costumes, following on behind the band. It simply will not work, the main business here is speed, surely a liability in both bands and drum majorettes.

Before they go around the brickyard in Indianapolis, the build-up is of course not only an adjunct, but a necessity. It is such a boring race you see. They simply go round and round a banked oval. On the Isle of Man, ultimately, the riders race not one another, but striving for perfection, they race against themselves. Any pre-race extravanganzas would be a distraction.

All the competitiors that I spoke to on the Island were fascinated by the race; each gave me his reasons for coming. Jack Findlay, Australian and then a works Suzuki rider and world championship contender, slim and curiously still, drawled, 'I'm here because this race sharpens me for all the rest and that's the truth. If I do O.K.

here I'm O.K. for the rest of the season.'
He did however complain that the race was not well enough publi-
cized throughout the world and with this I am in complete agree-
ment. This is where the hoopla is really needed Mr Chairman, not
prior to the race.
'They could have 'em falling off the bloody pier if they half tried.'
I almost expected him to add 'digger' or 'bazza'.

   His team mate Paul Smart, serious, sitting next to his very hot,
very fast factory-built special, concurred.
'I enjoy the T.T.' then a pause, 'except when it rains, then I hate it.'
His last utterance was curiously angry.
Later I listened to a T.T. veteran holding forth.
'Can't understand these young fellas, we used to race come rain,
sleet or shine. Too much molly coddling. Now in my day . . . . '
None of the riders standing round the upright, white-haired old
man, pointed out that his bike could do 50 mph, while theirs',
.without exception, could top 150 mph.

   Mick Grant, another world class rider, who prosaically lists his
profession as 'Motorcyclist', was more adamant.
'It's the finest race in the world — unconditionally, the name of the
game is road racing, not circuit.'
The ginger-haired Yorkshireman chewed a little on his red
moustache, 'You could say I luv the Isle of Man.'

A side car rider, Ron Coxon, belly bulging into his vest and out of
his oily trousers replied with Northern bluntness, 'Why do I cum
here? Because I'm a bloody twat, that's why. Its self inflicted
pissin' torture.'
To hear him tell it the agony far outweighed the ecstasy, yet he
had done thirteen T.T.'s to date and the closest he had come to
winning was fifteenth, a feat he repeated in a later race. He had
just installed a new engine in his combination, the reason being, he
added, 'Te bring joy inter the twilight of me life.'

I realized then that I was talking to a man with his roots deep in both racing and vaudeville.

Early, very early one morning, with the sun just rising and almost everyone on the Island asleep, I spoke to Charlie Williams. 'I have to ride hard, but within my limits, because the scenery is different here you know. You use a different technique . . . . and it's more important for me to win here than anywhere else.' Because I was untutored in the race world I asked him another question.
'Have you raced here before?'
He smiled gently at me.
'I won last year's International Lightweight race and the 250 Production and I came third in the Formula 750 . . . .'

The seagulls were swooping and diving overhead and the clouds pink and beautiful, sat lightly on the crisp, clear dawn.

There are of course some people who genuinely dislike the Isle of Man races. Rod Gould, an ex-world champion and now effective manager of the European Yamaha racing team was direct when he refused to race there anymore.
'I'm a rider, not a bloody hero.'
Now he refuses to allow the Yamaha works team to race here. Jack Findlay added,
'Ago (Giacomo Agostini, legendary world champion) would be here like a shot you know, he needs the world championship points but old Rod won't let him.'
Agostini lost the world championship at year's end.

In the paddock, the solos were back and the last of the sidecars was preparing to go out on the track. Whatever your thoughts or feelings you get bound up with the excitement and the tension. The chief timekeeper, Stan Nicholls, as a special dispensation, allowed me into the timekeepers' box, 'Provided you don't say *anyting* at *any time*.' Considering the all - encompassing ear - shattering noise, this seemed an unnecessary embargo. An electric light, dangling nakedly in front of the wide window facing the starting grid, blinked on and the last sidecar was away. While we waited for the rest to come back in, Stan talked to me.

'I used to race before the war, but then I got married and it's not a married man's game, so I got into timekeeping and now I've reached the top of the ladder.'

I, as ordered, said nothing.

With the sun making long shadows, the last of the sidecars came in under its own power and a few more were towed in. In a marquee reserved for riders and officials the hubbub was incredible as riders and passengers relived the day's excitement.

'. . . . flat in top . . . . sprocket off . . . . misfire . . . crack in frame . . . . you'll not believe this . . . . Christ you can't on Governors . . . eight and a half . . . . you fucking liar, 'scuse my English . . . argon weld . . . .'

I walked out swamped by language and dazed by intensity and event. No one had mentioned the previous day's accident. As I was looking for a lift to the sea front I recognized another rider whom I knew, John Cowie. I had met him first at Brands Hatch, he was one of the Gus Kuhn, Norton riders. He had told me he was to race in his first T.T. Then his young face smiled and his eyes twinkled behind his spectacles. He had pulled on his space-age crashhelmet and long hair dancing wildly behind him, had disappeared in a howl of noise. Now in the comparative silence he was scowling.

'Hello.'

'Hello.'

'How's it going?'

'I'm not racing.'

'Why?'

'Fell off at Mallory, hurt my leg. *Can't* ride.'

The high point of his year had disappeared.

'Well that's the way it is.'

He limped painfully away. Then he turned around and there was a flash of the former smile.

Chapter 1

'You enjoying yourself?'

'It's blowing my mind,' I said truthfully.

'Practice again tomorrow starts round four in the morning.'

Now his smile was broader.

'You will be here won't you?'

I was very tired, limp from too many sensations and my leg, mangled in a long ago car accident, was hurting most painfully. I doubted whether I could make the evening, let alone some pagan hour the following morning.

'Well?'

'Oh yes, I'll be here.'

An old Catholic reflex of praying to God in time of trouble almost crept up, I was that defenceless.

The liming rider smiled broadly, 'See you then.'

Dear God . . . .

Chapter 2

'Me old man doesn't like the races so he goes to Blackpool with the kids and I come over to T.T.'

Housewife

My fascination with the race started with a picture on a wall. The entrance to the house in which I grew up was notable for two things. Immediately on opening the front door, one was confronted by a large, dusty, bewhiskered, stuffed Wildebeest head. This looked down on everything with a glazed malevolence. Below it was a picture of a motorcycle racer, an uncle of mine, and his mechanic. They both affected an air of nonchalance in front of a 'Velocette' motorcycle. The uncle was wearing racing leathers and his goggles were slung carelessly around his neck. The mechanic was immaculate in white overalls with the regulation rag hanging from a back pocket. Only a battered tin of Castrol oil in one corner intruded on the posed orderliness. I used to gaze at the photograph for hours. The inscription on the bottom read simply 'T.T. races, 1935'. My speculation and dreams about the race in another land were curtailed abruptly when termites, a concomitant of the sub-tropical climate in which we lived, devoured the wall surrounding the Wildebeest's head and it came crashing down, demolishing the photograph in the process. The termites poured hurriedly out of the broken nose of the Wildebeest and my mother made plans to sell the house before it too fell to pieces. I went back to reading another uncle's copies of 'Motor Cycle' and 'Motorcycling'. These journals, unlike their modern counterparts, were middle class, sometimes boring and always entirely respectable. They contained long pieces with complicated equations, dealing with cornering on a motorcycle, was it better to lean with or away from the motorcycle? Centres of gravity, coefficients of friction and castor angles were gravely discussed by people who signed off with M.Inst.Mech.Eng., Dip.Tech. (Mech.Eng.), Fel.Mech.Eng. Soc. and so on. There were exploded drawings of the insides of

17

Chapter 2

motorcycle engines, meticulously detailed, logical and beautiful.
Both uncles to my regret, forsook motorcycles more or less simultaneously. The one took to drink, the other to flying atom
bombers from A to B. It is difficult to decide which was the more
useless occupation.

Years later, as a television producer, I tried to do a documentary
on the Isle of Man T.T. races. The T.V. executives' reactions were
unexpected.
'No one is interested in bloody motorcycles anymore. Now last
week I said to Jackie Stewart . . . .'
'The T.T.! Good God, I thought they'd stopped it years ago.'
When I left the B.B.C. for daring to question the veracity of some
news broadcasts, I suddenly had the freedom to do as I wanted. I
decided to explore my old fascination, the world of the T.T. and
the racers.

Liverpool was, as always, shrouded in drizzle. Near the ferry-
boat hundreds of motorcycles snarled and roared. Then when it
seemed that one of them must explode from too much anticipa-
tion, a secret signal was given and they surged aboard. A few more
final roars while the riders parked, then they inspected the com-
petition. An M.V. Agusta 750 S was clearly the centre of attraction.
The proud owner dispensed statistics.
'Cost £2,400.'
Collective whistle.
'Can top one hundred and fifty.'
Mute admiration. One woman touched it experimentally.
'Oh it sends shivers up me just looking at it,' she said with a sexual
sigh. Her boyfriend pulled her away from the mechanical Don
Juan.

The racing riders arrived more prosaically in Transit vans, their
racing machines shrouded from prying eyes. The sidecar combinations on trailers were similarly hooded.

The ferry passengers were a leather fetishist's dream. Never-endingly the motorcyclists and their girlfriends trudged around the boat in leather boots, tight leather trousers, leather jackets and leather gloves. They had another distinguishing mark. They were coated in a thin film of engine oil. The racers in contrast were modishly dressed and none had oil anywhere. I joined Stan Woods, John Williams (two competitors) and their mechanics for a drink. As we put to sea the bikers came down to identify their heroes. 'That's Barry Sheene.'
Almost right, it was his mechanic.
Stan and John sipped carefully on their beers as the Queens 1st Leather Lancers stomped up to the bar and with much machismo, ordered fizzy orange.

The talk of the racers was of engines. Any engines, all engines. 'That bloody Transit of mine is doing about ten to the gallon.'
'You need a good mechanic to tune it.'
'Can't get one.'
The mechanic who had spent years tuning engines to unimaginable peaks, smiled.
Stan Woods did not look like a world class rider, more like a man who had spent years learning an ancient and obscure craft like Follet Gilding or Napsmithing. Everything about him was controlled. He moved carefully and spoke sparingly. I had seen him racing the previous day at Brands Hatch. Man and machine were effortlessly one. I realized that he *was* a craftsman, and that his craft was not ancient, but the highly modern one of speed.

The mechanics tried to get him to buy a round of beer. Reluctantly he went to the bar.
'Mean old bugger, the first round he's bought in years.'
With his back to the speaker Stan shook the beer can vigorously and then handed it to him. He smiled pleasantly when the beer can exploded in his detractor's face.

There was little talk of the forthcoming races and a lot of

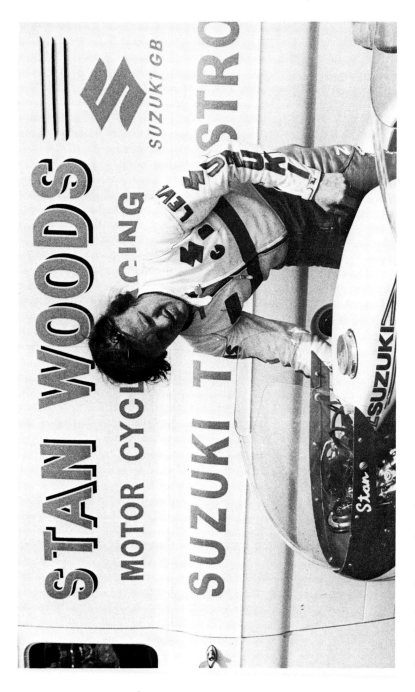

Stan Wood, craftsman of speed

mechanical details.

'How's the 350?'

'Not happy with the handling — need a new damper on the steering.'

'My back suspension's playing up.'

It was difficult for me to realize that these men would soon be competing relentlessly against each other. They talked of absent riders.

'That Sheeny is on a total ego trip you know. Even tape recorded the interview he did on radio Lux.'

'What's he going to do with it?'

'Save it for posterity.'

Laughter.

The mechanics drank more beer. The riders were still on their first pints. By now the ship was well into the Irish sea and I was feeling distinctly queasy.

'Let's go and have a nice big steak — got work to do this afternoon,' said John Williams. He was referring to the fact that soon after landing on the Isle of Man they would be practising at high speed. Both he and Stan Woods had been at Brands Hatch the previous day, raced, packed up and driven to Liverpool. I had come by train, and even so I was feeling tired. The sea added to my discomfort. They, on the other hand, seemed full of rude health and animal laughter.

I went up to the upper deck to get some fresh air. I carefully chose a seat next to a woman with jet black hair and large round breasts. She immediately puked on my shoes and apologized limply. I moved. A father and child puked ahead of me. I found a quiet spot near a machine that chewed up rubbish and spat it into the sea. Every now and again a sailor with a mop and bucket would slosh water between the doubled up people and mop the vomit away. He obligingly mopped my shoes.

To my infinite delight Douglas was rock steady and bathed in warm sunshine. The holiday makers and motorcycle fans poured off the ferry and on to the promenade. The roar of the motor-cycles contrasted oddly with the steady clip clop of the horse-drawn trams on the sea front. It is incidentally the only public transport in Britain which makes an unsubsidized profit. Some £3,000 per annum.

The Isle of Man has always been a resort for working class Northerners, a sort of slightly classier Blackpool. It is tiny, about ten miles across and thirty miles long. A Tourist Board official told me that the Isle of Man 'had a Gulf Stream climate'. He pointed out two bedraggled palm trees to support his theory. Remembering Ernest Hemingway's vivid description of fishing for marlin in the Gulf Stream, with the sun almost an enemy, it occurred to me that one or the other was a liar.

The Isle of Man has erratic and it would seem, totally unpredictable weather.
'All we get from across the Irish Sea is the bloody rain and the bloody Irish,' observed one Manxman.
The T.T. races started on the Isle of Man because it has a semi-autonomous parliamentary system within the United Kingdom. When Britain, or rather England, decreed that there should be no roads closed for the purposes of racing and indeed that there should be no racing, the Manxmen passed a bill allowing both road closure and racing. This was the beginning of the Isle of Man Tourist Trophy. To celebrate the event the polysyllabically named Marquis de Mouzilly St. Mars in 1907 donated a statuette, Mercury, balancing precariously on a motorcycle wheel. But as with all statues, the more incongruous they are, the higher their status.

In the early days the motorcycles were rated at three and a half horse power, the track record was 38 mph and the fuel consumption was some 90 miles per gallon. Nowadays the team Suzuki kicks out about one hundred horse power, the track record is nudging 110 mph and they gulp fuel at 14 miles per gallon. During practice and races the roads leading to and forming part of the circuit are closed. Nothing except the riders (and the occasional cat as noted) is allowed on the road. You are not allowed to walk, run or jump across the main road. The Islanders surprisingly accept this prohibition with equanimity. The only sign of minor irritation I saw on the part of an Islander was a sign 'This is *private* property. Keep off, specially during the race.' Considering the number of speed-drunk spectators climbing over and through everything to reach the best vantage point, I was not surprised.

The Islanders number some 40,000 in all. During the summer there are a half a million visitors and it has the highest concentration of motorcycles per square mile in the world over T.T. week. I regret to say that if a visitor is unaccustomed to eating between 1 and 2 pm and 6 and 7 pm and dislikes fish and chips he or she will starve. On the Island, boarding house eating hours are strictly observed. Even the most hardened biker disappears over these periods to eat. On the brighter side, the pubs stay open all day, serve Irish draught Guinness (no matter what they say, a markedly different drink from that brewed and served in Britain) and the products of the two local breweries. These two brews, while better than Watneys (but then I am informed that even gnats piss is better than Watneys) are not in the Greene King or Gale's Ales class.

While I'm off motorcycles for a minute I can also unreservedly recommend Manx ice cream. By law it is ice cream like it used to be. None of your polyunsaturated fats, animal fats, emulsifier and certified colouring and flavouring, but egg, milk and cream. Its probably easy to make as well.

Part of the charm of the Isle of Man for me was that it is, I suspect, what rural Britain used to be. There are leafy lanes with unimaginable smells of wild flowers, clear tinkling streams without algae, rusty tins or old motor cars. The beaches are clear and clean with no oil on them. Everyone knows one another and there is an easy-going air which is noticeable the moment one steps ashore in Douglas. Indeed the traffic safety officer was at pains to try and educate the locals in the habits of the visitors.

'They're used to a slower pace you see. They get bewildered by the fast pace of the visitors.'

Most of the motorcycle visitors zipping around the Island are bent on imitating their chosen race heroes and a less tolerant society would lock the majority of them up — for their own safety. One night I saw a slightly drunken biker push-start his unbaffled Gilera to life racing style, and roar up and down the promenade without lights on. ('So the coppers can't take his number,' confided his mate.) He was doing well over a hundred miles an hour on the promenade and his friends raised a ragged cheer every time he roared past.

The police are large, stolid and considering the long hours they work over the T.T. period, remarkably even-tempered. One I spoke to was adamant about the race and the spectators.

'Never any trouble I tell you. Main trouble is,' here he paused and looked around, 'main trouble is the Irish.' He looked around again and dropped his voice, 'Also we have Scots week. All the Scotties come over. Then it's the Irish *and* the Scots. Unbelievable!'

I must visit the Island one Scots week. Might even make a good book.

The Manxman's view of himself is one of unblemished virtue. They are (according to themselves) hard working, generous to a fault and set a pattern of national budgetary control via capitalism and free enterprise that the rest of Britain, or indeed the world, would do well to emulate. Unfortunately us shiftless lot lack the ability to work as hard etc. etc. The one fault with this thesis is as every Islander knows, they work only six months a year, when the tourists arrive. The rest of the year is spent in cheerful socializing. Having said that the Island is totally geared to tourism, I must add that the Islanders are the most honest people I have ever come across. The pretty, penny pinching cheating, all pervasive in Britain, is totally absent on the Island. May it remain so.

The Island then revolves around four T's — Tourism, the T.T. and T.V. Some newer inhabitants find this boring, others restful.

Driving around the island I happened to hear a news item. Dr Niklaus Pevsner who has with Teutonic thoroughness looked upon and written about every building in Britain, is about to do the same for the Isle of Man, thus completing his magnum opus. I am interested to know what he makes of the architecture here. To me it seemed to vary from classic (Henry the Horrible) to modern (Mies van der Terrible) with nothing in between. I am certain he will devote considerable scholarly effort to an analysis of Sarah's and Kate's cottages. I hope he remembers that they race past them.

Politically the Island embodies the essence of community politics — there are no real parties. Elections proceed on personalities (and some cash exchanges, although the latter was never mentioned). There is an underground political party 'Fo Halloo'. It is so well and deeply underground that no one knew about it. The one man who was a mine of information on it was a television reporter from Granada. He was a mine of information on a large number of other subjects, all of which subsequently turned out to be incorrect. Beware Lancastrians, you are being misled.

Finally the tourists. The T.T. period is a W.A.S.P. celebration. I saw not one coloured over the entire period. Japanese (works Suzuki) yes, coloured, no. The men are a mixed lot, mostly Northerners. An old man with a tribal face at my hotel related his past to me, where he worked and how many years he had been coming to the Island. I referred to the white-haired woman sitting next to him as his wife. She glared at me and left.
'Aye lad, me missus passed on. That one's been cummin' 'ere as long as me. Never watches races. Tell the truth I don't know her front name. Miss Smales her surname. Good Northern name.'

The young women were bye and large peroxide blond, plump pouter pigeons, constantly licking icecream cones or eating fish and chips. They generally went around in pairs. The girls in leathers always had a man and a motorcycle near at hand. At the final prize-giving I did sit next to a housewife who said, 'Me old man doesn't like the races, so he goes to Blackpool with the kids and I come over to T.T.'

I stopped Charlie Williams and he obligingly signed her autograph book. For a moment that middle-aged housewife had all the characteristics of a teeny bopper getting Donny Osmond's signature.

'Oh I just don't know how to thank you luv. Wait till I show Doris, she'll be that jealous.'

Doris was her neighbour in Salford.

Another tourist, a muscular dental surgeon, who owned two vintage cars and four motorcycles allowed me to admire one of his motorcycles, a Vincent H.R.D. in mint condition. He explained how the suspension worked and how the engine formed part of the frame. And what was my interest? Well, I was writing a book on the T.T. He was amazed.

'If you don't mind my saying, your technical knowledge seems a little lacking, considering the complexity of modern motorcycles.' For once I came up with an on-the-spot comment that I am proud of.

'Perhaps the quality of my writing will compensate for the lacunae in my knowledge.'

Chapter 3

'It's the last of the real races . . . .'
Veteran T.T. rider

If the spectators are enthusiasts the veteran riders are fanatics. They come back year after year to meet, exchange gossip and generally depore the fact that man, machine and race have gone to the dogs since they last raced. Some 'last races' go back very far indeed, to the nineteen twenties. Inside the veterans' tent was another, older world. Whiskey in hand, they were as fast with opinions as they once were on their motorcycles. One old rider commented on the winner of the Senior T.T. race.
'Well not as stylish as Frith or Duke, but I suppose he'll have to do . . . .'

The photographs on the wall were of motorcycles gone forever. Long stroke engines, brakes something like the caliper brakes used nowadays on bicycles. The riders, caught in the moment before they set off, all wore leather helmets of the type favoured by early pilots and their begoggled eyes looked sternly into the middle distance. A spare tyre slung like a bandolier over their shoulders and a myriad of spanners and spares tucked in everywhere completed the ensemble. It has always been a tough, long race, but then apparently you had to be prepared not only for the worst but for something approximating to the apocalypse.

Sitting beneath the photographs I chatted to some of the men, now changed by time but with memories still surprisingly clear. 'In the old days the roads were terrible. Sometimes it was better to get off them. I remember a section on the mountain where it was quicker to take a path than the road. And at Creg (Creg-ny-Baa, a famous right-angled corner) there was a stream running across the road.'

Alec Fraser, a thin, upright stick of a man, 78 years old, raced in 1923, on an OEC Blackburne. This was his fifty first visit. He gave the latter information without any hesitation. Then there were rigid frames, bad roads, brakes that only just worked and cows wandering all over the roads. He was adamant that the race was easier nowadays.

'Look at them, as comfortable as wheel-chairs. Another thing, in my day it was an honour to be accepted as a rider. Now they want to be paid. I ask you!'

His voice rose with indignation.

'Still, I suppose some things haven't changed,' he continued. 'In my day there was this and Brooklands, that was just like the circuit races at Brands. We used to call Brooklands the millpond. Compared to here it was. You see,' here he looked at me earnestly, almost begging for total sympathetic comprehension, 'it's the last of the real races . . . . all the others have gone, changed. It can't be bettered. I wish people would understand that.'

Another veteran was scornful of the absent world champion, Phil Read.

'You know he was here and an old rider asked him how much he had made out of racing. He said over a hundred thousand pounds and do you know what, his wife turned around and said, "Come on, let's go, what does this old duffer know about racing." So they left. We rode for enjoyment — we also had better manners.'

Reg Thompson, a bluff Yorkshireman looked at me judiciously, 'And you can quote me on that.'

Norman Scott organizes the veterans' club. You have to have started in the T.T. to become a member and you have to be male. Since only very few women have taken part in the T.T. as sidecar passengers, but never as riders, this may not seem unreasonable. However Russians send women into outer space and I was told an American woman would be entering for the next Junior T.T. Why then this male chauvinism? Norman adjusted his cap, carefully stuck full of trout flies and cleared his throat.

Mike the bike

Chapter 3

'Well it's a bit difficult you see. We have an annual dinner in
London.'
'So?'
'Well at the dinner they tell jokes . . . .'
'Ah, a stag evening.'
'Yes, that's it. Sort of upper class stag evening. Don't want to
offend the women now do we.'
Chivalrous to the end.

One veteran in impeccable Eton-accented English, entertained
me with the latest gossip from the Palace (Buck House, as he called
it) and retailed the exploits of one wealthy ex-rider.
'He's a bit queer you know. But then most intelligent people are,
don't you agree?'
He looked me in the eye. Whether challenging my intellect or my
sexual habits I shall never know.

I was dragged into a discussion as to whether widening and
smoothing some parts of the road, to the tune of some £100,000
per annum helped the race. The record set some years back by
Mike Hailwood still stood, despite faster bikes. This was used as a
proof that all further improvements were useless. With today's
powerful bikes perhaps this was a necessity I ventured. Rubbish,
the race was never safer. To hear them talk, the dead littered the
track in the good old days, a sure sign of good sport.

A very old ex-rider drove me back to my hotel. The journey was
interesting. It was a hot afternoon and the old man rolled down the
side window an inch, 'So the windscreen doesn't mist up'. He rev-
ved the engine until it was warm then slapping it into gear, took off
in a racing start. 'Just tell me where to go,' he said speeding for the
gate. On the way we overtook everything and he double declutched
whenever he changed gear. Charging up a hill he hooted at two
young motorcyclists. They turned round and regarded the octogen-
arian with amazement.

'Young pups, no idea now to drive,' he said as he whizzed past them. At the hotel I got out and thanked him nervously for the lift.
'Don't mention it, don't mention it. See you tomorrow.'
He was off again, rear wheels spinning, hunched over the steering wheel.

Outside the veterans' marquee the next day I saw the man who is probably Britain's most famous rider: Geoffrey Duke, six times world champion in the early fifties and undeniably one of the most stylish riders ever to race.

An old man approached him with an autograph book. Geoff Duke signed obligingly and handed it back to the old man. The old man then handed it to his grandson.
'Now tha's got a *real* one there lad.'
The young boy goggled at the great name.

When they were out of earshot Duke turned to his son and with genuine astonishment said,
'It's amazing, I haven't ridden for years and they still recognize me.'
He shook his head at the thought. He was also, as a rider informed me, 'the last of the gentleman riders, he wouldn't cut in front of you if there was any chance of that causing an upset or accident.'

He perfected a style of riding that was at the same time beautiful to watch and extremely fast.
'I always rode with my machine. I had the idea that man and machine should become one.'
I recalled a very old film I had seen of him whipping around a corner, he and the bike tilted over to the limit, in one beautiful fast line. There was only one problem, a telegraph pole was in the way, which, were he to continue, would surely decapitate him. With all the casual elegance and split second timing of a natural athlete, he flicked his head up, missing the pole by a fraction and then ducked back again. All this at well over a hundred miles an

hour without the line of his bike or body altering a jot.
'Where was that,' I asked him, 'Zandvoort?'
'No it was here actually, near Ginger Hall. They took the pole away
eventually, bit worried that someone might try my trick and fail.'
He smiled at the idea of his old skill.

At fifty one, Geoffrey Duke, O.B.E., now lives on the Isle of
Man. This worried me a little because I once worked with a television executive, Donald Baverstock, who was so enmeshed with his
triumphs in the distant past, that he had extreme difficulty coping
with the present. I asked Geoff Duke why he lived on the Isle of
Man, was it to be near the scene of his past triumphs? He dismissed
this question quickly and easily. He was here simply because he
liked the Isle of Man and its inhabitants and his business, selling
motor spares to the trade, was here. There is a quality about him
which I noticed in all of the best riders, an air of pervasive tranquil-
lity. Polite and thoughtful, he spoke to me in his office, one wall of
which was loaded with more cups and trophies than I had ever
seen.
'No, these are not all. They're the overflow. The rest are at home,'
he remarked diffidently.

He learnt to ride as a dispatch rider during the war and ended up
as an instructor. He first came over to the Isle of Man to race in
the 1948 Manx Grand Prix. This race, run over the same course as
the T.T., is an amateur's version of the T.T. (Paul Smart, works
Suzuki rider, was more brusque in his description of the Manx G.P.
'Full of a crowd of bloody Wallies!') Duke came over with his
privately owned Norton and booked in at a modest hotel. 'It was
12/6 a day all found.' He got a young boy to help him as a mechanic. (Years later he discovered that the young boy, with true Manx
dedication to racing, had played truant for the entire period.) He
set about learning the circuit.
'I split the circuit up into three and I would take my road motorcycle out and go over every bend. I'd stop, look at it and remember
it, forwards and backwards. When I was happy with one section

I'd go on to the next.'
In this way he memorized intimately all the subtleties and nuances
of well over a hundred twists and bends on the thirty seven mile
circuit.
'The surface was a bit rougher in those days, but not as bad as the
old timers say.'
Every night after practice, Duke and his young mechanic would
check and clean his racing bike, then he would go out to re-visit
the corners he was not sure of. He never consulted with the other
riders, he was always very much a loner and he relied on his
memory, never any notes, for a precise topology of the Isle of Man
circuit.
'I was lucky, I seemed to have a good memory for the circuit.'

This is another trait that he shares with all world class riders.
They have a precise, almost mathematical knowledge, not just of
the bends in a circuit, but the small imprecise bumps that abound
on every road and are unnoticed by the average driver passing over
them at 30 mph. At 130 mph that same imperceptible bump will
ensure that you become airborne if you are not very careful. This
feat, of memorizing the road and the line to take on the Isle of
Man, is roughly comparable to memorizing an entire book, word
perfect. Not only this, but there are other tracks, Imola, Nurburg-
ring, Auvergne, Salzburg, to mention only a few of the world
championship road circuits. I remembered Stirling Moss, the motor
car racer, recounting how he and his navigator Jenkinson, planned
his victory in the 1955 Mille Miglia, a race going all the way through
Italy. This road race had been totally dominated by Italians, for
not only did they have good racing cars — they knew the winding
tortuous route of the race better than anyone else. Moss and
Jenkinson planned to beat them. They drove and re-drove relentlessly over the long road, evolving a system of signals from navigator to driver to warn him of what was ahead. They would practise
their signals in their hotel room at night.
'Short straight, third, brake at post, fast right hander . . . I'm sorry,
it was a left hander.'

Chapter 3

There was a painful silence.
'I said I'm sorry.'
'It's no use, we would have been doing a hundred and fifty miles
an hour. We are both dead,' said Moss.
This is what mistakes or loss of memory do in a race.
So with meticulous care all the best riders learn the circuits and in
particular the longest and the most difficult of them all, the Isle of
Man.

Duke returned in 1949 and despite an accident came second in
the 350cc Manx G.P. and in 1950 he joined the works Norton
team. This is when he started winning world championships. He
also had behind him a designer of genius, Rod McCandlass, who
evolved the 'Featherbed Norton', virtually tailormade for Duke and
his riding style. Even today Geoff Duke has firm ideas on design
and what changes to make on a motorcycle to get the best out of
it. This trait is conspicuous by its absence in the present generation
of works riders. They commented on the handling of their machines, sometimes acidly, but were unable to offer concrete mechanical suggestions as to how their problems should be overcome. Perhaps the technology has now advanced so far that only the specialists are capable of coping with their own little niche.
('I do timing,' said one mechanic, 'he does the frame, suspension
and all that and he,' indicating a third, 'looks after the engine.'
This bike, I should add, failed to start on race day.)

In 1951 and 1952 Geoff Duke won three world championships
in the 350 and 500cc class and then he left Norton for Gilera. I
can still remember the shock with which I assimilated the news as
a child. Duke had betrayed us, he had not only left Norton, he had
joined the dreaded Eyeties.
'After 1952 I could no longer win on a Norton. They had frozen
their design. It was better for a Briton to win on a Gilera than lose
on a Norton.'
So this patriotic British rider with his ingrained Northern habits
went over to the Italians.

'They treated me like one of the family you know. The only trouble in the first year was the food. But then I got used to that, canelloni and all that and now I rather miss it.'

Last year Gilera sent over the bike that he won the 1955, 500cc world championship on and he did a tour of the circuit.

'It was exactly as I left it, dirty plugs and all. I put in some clean oil and we were away. Gear box was a bit sticky though. Ballaugh (a hump backed bridge where everyone slows down and nevertheless becomes airborne for some thirty or more startling feet) in third was interesting.'

The understatement was characteristic. The tour on his old bike had reawakened no unrequited hopes or desires. He had ridden hard and indisputably well in his race career. He stopped 'when it became no longer a joy. I did one hundred and sixty eight laps in Locarno in 1959. I won the 250, 350 and 500cc races and I was totally worn out in the end. That was the day I decided to stop.'

We spoke about racing in general. The carefree atmosphere of former times had changed and a new breed of businessmen/riders were becoming prominent. We also spoke about the danger and death in racing.

'Well like everyone else I always thought it would never happen to me.'

In his case he was correct, his only major accident, in which he ripped open his rib cage and ruptured a lung, was in a racing motor car. All that ever happened to him on a motorcycle was a minor leg injury which he discovered some three months later was actually a fracture. Also, he only fell off once in the T.T. race at Quarter Bridge.

'I hit some melted tar and the back stepped out. The bike slid away and ripped the fuel tank. If it wasn't for that I could have carried on.'

With sad precision he ticked off all his contemporaries who had been killed racing motorcycles — Amm, Bell, Hartle, McIntyre, Ivy, Graham. Then he was perfectly still and silent while he waited for my next question.

Chapter 3

Because I was with the master, the man who really elevated motorcycle racing from a sport into an art, I had to ask him one final question, in the hope that his skill, his talents would somehow, however uselessly, rub off on me.

'What makes a world championship rider?'

He paused for a while before answering.

'That's a difficult one. To begin with you must have the right temperament. Not too excitable. I've got very low blood pressure so that when I was racing it probably went up to normal.'

He looked at his 'overflow' trophies.

'You need good eyesight, mine used to be exceptional — but not now . . . . Stamina, judgement, oh yes and a delicacy of control. A lot of people don't appreciate that. An ability to ride on the limit, and a knowledge of what the limit is. Quick reflexes, but more important, you must be able to work things out quickly under pressure.'

Then he smiled at me.

'You also need flair.'

Yes that was it. That indefinable something, something that cannot be taught, something which one man in a million will have — 'Flair'.

Chapter 4

'We're beat before we start.'
Mechanic working on Norton motorcycle

The modern racing solo motorcycles bear about as much resemblance to an everyday road machine as a 'dray horse to a race horse', to quote a rider. The solos use die-cast magnesium alloy wheels, hydraulic disc brakes front and rear, six gears, special suspension and steering dampers. But the main difference is in the engines. They have a small power band and the power comes in fiercely and quickly. These engines, two-strokes turning over at between eight and eleven thousand revolutions per minute, are purpose built, in fact they *cannot* be run slowly; allow their revs to drop and their plugs oil up, their heat balance changes and they cough and splutter most horribly. The men who tune these engines, pushing them to the limit of what metal can take, are obviously specialists.

Some of the riders are obliged to tune their own motorcycles, with help from friends and enthusiasts and some are able to hire their own 'spannermen'. They sometimes work excruciatingly long hours, three days and nights non-stop is not unknown and then at the end of all this care and attention, they hand the machines to another man who proceeds to do his best to ride it into the ground.

Early one morning I stopped Jack Findlay, of the Suzuki works team, elegant in blue leathers and fur lined parka. He paced about in solitary introspection, just prior to practising.
'How's the bike?'
'I don't know, that's what I aim to find out.'
He had had trouble with the frame. The engine was generating enough power to bend the normally straight frame out of line by the force it was exerting on the rear wheel via the chain drive.

Chapter 4

At high speeds this was making the bike virtually unmanageable and very dangerous. The Japanese team manager had contacted Japan and a new, stronger frame had been designed from scratch. It had been made and flown over to the Island. His mechanics had worked through the night to fit the engine in the new frame.
'How are the Japanese mechanics?'
Jack stopped walking and thought for a while.
'Well I'll tell you something. They work a bloody sight harder than us buggers and that's the truth.'
His blue eyes creased in a slight smile and he walked off again on his own.

To me it was interesting that the Suzuki team could get a completely new frame designed, made and shipped out to them in a few days. A mechanic I had spoken to previously, working on a Norton, was gloomy.
'It takes me three weeks to get a chrome-plated nut. We're beat before we start.'
Then he cheered up a little.
'Only chance we've got is if the opposition breaks down.'
Yet still this man worked, using all his skill and dedication to prepare the motorcycle.

Speaking to Jack Findlay later, after practice, when the new frame had proved a big improvement over the old, he elaborated on his ideas about his mechanics.
'There's a chief mechanic and then one for suspension and so on, but the difference between them and other mechanics I've had is that they feel a personal sense of responsibility to Mr Suzuki to see that the bit they're working on doesn't fail.'
Findlay had, in the early days, like all beginners, tuned his own motorcycles; we talked about that.
'I had a Bultaco I used to race.'
'How are they?'
He smiled at the memory of working too hard all night and racing too fast during the day.

'Oh they're good. They have a tendency to go very fast.'
A delicate pause. 'They also have a tendency to sieze, throwing you
on the road very rapidly, which is interesting.'
His team mate Paul Smart also once rode Bultacos.
'Death on two wheels,' he said succinctly.

It was odd talking to Findlay and Smart in their garages. The
mechanics talked loudly in Japanese, a language which sounds very
much like a sergeant major's short rasping barks, albeit a little
more nasal and in the background, going full blast, was an expensive transistor radio, belting out the latest pop song, which they
would hum intermittently. My only question to one of them was
met by a polite smile. Inscrutable bugger I thought. The chief
mechanic interrupted,
'He does not understand English please.'

Watching other mechanics at work, in just about every alley and
garage in Douglas and marvelling at their manual dexterity, I
remembered a mechanic who had helped me years ago. It was
Christmas Eve and I got him out of a party to repair a bent valve.
He was very drunk, so drunk that he didn't bother to try and focus
his eyes on what he was doing. Instead, he knelt down and working by touch, barked out instructions to his assistant.
'Quarter Allen . . . . half inch socket . . . . screw driver . . . . three
quarter fixed . . . .'
The tools were slapped into the outstretched palm much the same
as a surgeon. When he was finished with the tool, he would drop it,
his assistant would retrieve it and await the next instruction.
'Three quarter nut . . . . no Whit not AF you p*!.. . . .'
He removed a cylinder head, took out the bent valve, did a quick
regrind, fixed the valve spring in position and bolted the head
back on again — all in about half an hour.
'What's he like when he's sober?' I asked his helper.
'Well that doesn't happen very often . . . .'

Most good mechanics have this gift of being able to work

incredibly fast. I was in a garage three hours before the start of the Junior T.T. race and one of the competitor's engines was spread out, literally in thousands of pieces, on the floor. The rider was helping the mechanic.

'Will you make it?'

There was not the slightest hesitation.

'Of course,' said the rider.

It once took me two months to assemble an engine and then it would not start. The mechanic here worked on without pausing, then said somewhat plaintively, 'I'm hungry.'

Fish and chips were brought in and he ate as he worked.

'Engine oil gives a funny taste to the chips,' was his only comment.

Every night of the week, no matter what the other attractions in some garage there would be a mechanic working patiently on an engine. With an extremely jolly party going on in a hotel about a hundred yards away, I watched a mechanic working in a garage under Manx Radio, meticulously strip a large Honda engine and examine the exhaust valves.

He was besieged by people leaving the party with the usual drunken hilarity, which, when one is sober, is remarkably unfunny. He carried on unperturbed. When I returned at three in the morning, he was still at it, striving for ultimate perfection.

After the Senior Race for 500cc machines, I was driving back to the Grandstand when I recognized the Transit that Mick Grant had been using. Since I had been particularly interested in Mick and he had failed to appear on lap one, I wanted to know the reasons for failure. A grim-lipped mechanic climbed out of the Transit.

'What went wrong?'

He ignored me. Since he knew me, I persisted.

'What went wrong?'

He exploded in exasperation.

'I don't know. Bloody bitch thing.'

He kicked the bike malevolently, then loaded it angrily into the

Transit and drove off. He was obviously as emotionally involved in winning or losing as any rider.

The other rider/mechanics are the sidecar riders and their passengers. Sidecar combinations have changed a great deal in design over the past years. Gone are the days when you strapped an extra wheel on the largest motorcycle available and entered a race. The 'chair' of today tends to be low, about eighteen inches high, with wide, small diameter wheels and an exotic variety of engines. These vary from hotted-up motorcycle power units, to motor car and even motor-boat engines. Since it is virtually impossible to buy a sidecar combination off the shelf, as you can a solo racer, all machines are handmade by the rider, usually with assistance from the passenger. This not only ensures that the combination is tailor-made for rider and passenger but also excludes anyone but the rider/builder from being the mechanic. The reason for this is simply that a stranger would be bewildered by the very individual layout of cables, pumps, pipes and brackets on each machine. With such an exotic blend, a lot can and often does go wrong. A scrutineer told me,
'They'e the ones we've really got to watch. Some of the mechanical tricks they get up to are positively lethal.'

However streamlined the sidecars look, they seemed to me to be very uncomfortable. The rider kneels over the engine, usually with his chest close to the cylinder head and the passenger throws him or herself around as gravity dictates.
I spoke to Alan Sansum.
'Is it comfortable?'
'Yes.'
'What's that bruise on your chest?'
'That's where the carbs hit me.'
'And the burn on your arm?'
'That was the exhaust.'
'But it's comfortable?'
'Yes, of course.'

Helper with time board

The solo riders tend to look down a little on the sidecar competitors.

'I mean Ron look at them, always full of grease, always poking around in their bleedin' engines, always breaking down. They're just glorified grease monkeys. Not real racers.'

Despite this, or perhaps because of it, I found them generally to be the most co-operative of all the competitors on the Isle of Man. They were certain that their contribution to the T.T. races was unique.

'Let's face it, no one would come to the Isle of Man to watch those solo boys going round, like a lot of clockwork dummies. We're the big attraction. Main problem is money. We need more money than the solos.'

Supporting the mechanics and riders were the various technical experts from the oil companies, chain companies, tyre companies and so on. I watched the 'Champion' spark plug technician examine a plug.

'Too rich I think. Jet it down a couple. You need a hotter plug as well.'

The thin rider in his leathers scowled and produced the exact price of a new plug. His girlfriend at his side, was obviously as worried as he was, at what the race was costing.

'It can't be helped, you must have one.'

Rather like discussing whether or not a child needed shoes.

Tony Mayhew the spark plug man, opened a book and made mysterious entries in it. He replaced the book and the money in a shoe box. I worked out that he was noting what type of plug he sold to each rider and the condition of the old plug he had examined. I admired his method and complimented him on it. He blushed.

'Well, ahem . . . . actually all I'm doing is ah. . . . noting down the takings.'

'You mean all this is a sort of cash register?'

'Yes.'

For a brief moment I remembered the American Moon Shot from Nasa headquarters in Houston. There were hundreds of men in front of hundreds of monitor screens. Each screen was displaying numerical information from a particular part of the rocket. Any malfunction would be spotted, the data fed into a complicated programme, on an on-line, ultra-high speed computer, the problem would be analyzed and the solution or alternative solutions would come chattering out. Instant decision and action, with all the hardware, software, bright lights and as many T.V. cameras as possible watching. I gazed at the shoebox. As I said, this is a very British occasion.

'May I help you?' said Mayhew.

I explained that I was writing a book. Amazement registered on his face.

'You write?'

The implication was that I suffered from some sort of personality defect.

'Yes.'

A mechanic came up and showed him a spark plug.

'Excuse me . . . .'

Early one morning I visited the Dunlop tent where the bikes' tyre pressures were being checked and occasionally, new tyres fitted. The man in charge was tall and bespectacled, with 'Dunlop' (literally) written all over him.

'Listen mate, do you mind moving down wind,' said a rider to him. 'Why?'

'Well I've got to ride just now and I'm worried I'll get pissed on the smell of your breath.'

The man moved.

'Can't understand it,' he said seriously, 'only finished off two bottles of Canadian Club last night.' Then he corrected himself, 'this morning.'

In the crisp cold air the first of the Japanese two-strokes started its searing scream.

The race used to be totally dominated by British motorcycles, Norton, A.J.S., Matchless, B.S.A., Triumph and Velocette, to mention some of the better known names. Then there were Ariels, Vincents, Douglas and Royal Enfields and a hundred others, all great bikes in their day. There were some continental successes but then the British bike was not only successful on the Isle of Man, it was a world beater. A look at the entry now confirms that the field is almost entirely swamped by Japanese machines, very good, very fast. In fact, the Japanese bikes on the Isle of Man have reached a point in the Senior (500cc) and Formula 750, where additional power is useless. The riders of the machines generally have more power than they can usefully use already. What happened to our great motorcycle industry? Nowadays we field the John Player Norton-Villiers-Triumph, to give it its full name. This machine, a combination so to speak of lung cancer and outmoded power unit, is our pride and joy, it has to be, it is all we have left.

The causes for the decline of the British bike are many and varied, but in the main, they can be traced to huge profits pre- and post-war which were disbursed amongst what must be the most stupid managements of all time. This managerial tradition is un-happily still with us. Some time ago Norton-Villiers-Triumph (N.V.T.) decided to close a plant at Meriden in order to 'rationalize' their production. The workers at Meriden, with a trusting faith in the quality and craftsmanship of their product, demurred. They took the plant over and continued to make motorcycles, without the management. The managers of N.V.T. at this point, although guaranteed compensation, took this very badly. There was an air of 'how dare those louts succeed, where we, well-mannered, bred-to-lead men have failed'. To add insult to injury, Americans placed firm orders for the Meriden works output, which management did its best to block. Instead of being happy that these sales would further advertise their product overseas, N.V.T. placed a number of expensive advertisements in the press, decrying 'the Meriden factory blockade'. This statement was not only misleading but a gross inversion of the truth. On the next page the Japanese glossily extolled the virtues of their motorcycles. 'Let the good times roll.' The Meriden incident was to me, in a nutshell what has bedevilled the British motorcycle industry for years. It is run by a management more concerned with political and social theology than with designing and building better bikes.

On a personal level, all my initial letters to the Norton team wer were ignored. When I rang their headquarters, the lines were continually engaged. I was told cheerfully by another enthusiast that this was the normal state of affairs. On the Island, the John Player Norton team and their manager were always too busy to see me. When I did in fact walk into their garage it was the only time on the Island that I met with any hostility. The John Player Nortons, despite all the ballyhoo, came nowhere in any race. They broke down and a few days later a statement was issued, placing the blame implicitly on the miners. They had caused a beleaguered Prime Minister to declare a three day working week, which in turn forced Nortons to use an inferior piston, which cracked up on lap one.

In contrast to our shrunken industry, the Japanese took the market, at a time when every British manager in the motorcycle industry was talking about 'decline in demand'. Curiously enough, the Japanese followed their tradition in refining an existing product. What they also did was to give the motorcycle rider exactly what he or she wanted. They advertised their products extensively via racing. The engine, the ultra high revving two-stroke which was the breakthrough, existed already. This in itself is an interesting story.

In engine development there are generally two courses open to the design engineer. He can build an engine, change this, alter that, build another engine and another and another. The cost of this in terms of manpower, effort and finance is astronomical — also, the end result may, and has often been, a dismal failure. Lacking money, people sometimes have to make do with talent. This is precisely what an East German engineer, Walter Kaaden did. He sat down and worked out; theoretically, what was needed. This, leading as it did to exhaust and inlet resonances, disc valves, asymmetric timing, squish type combustion chamber and a whole host of technical innovations, is the engineering equivalent of being a Shakespeare. What is more, Kaaden's theoretical predictions were correct, and on a shoestring he built the MZ racer. His rider was Ernst Degner, himself an excellent mechanic. When the bike first came out it was clearly a world beater, but little known. The top names would have liked to ride it, but at the time East Germany was only paying riders in blocked currency, i.e. whatever you earn-ed had to be spent in East Germany. The Italians on the other hand were offering lire, 'real money'. The bike thus attracted engineering attention but little else. Then Degner defected — to Japan. In a few years the Japanese had refined the original MZ de-sign into the world beating Suzukis and Yamahas. Another interes-ting sidelight on sales is that this year's racing Yamaha is last year's factory team model. So, provided you can afford one, you stand a chance of being very close, in terms of machine capability, to the factory sponsored team.

Before the development of the very powerful two-strokes, Honda entered the field with modified four-stroke engines, once again improving a concept which had been 'proved useless' and dis-carded by British manufacturers. This engine involved a rearrange-ment and doubling up of the valves.

The arrival of the Japanese at the Isle of Man T.T. races in the late fifties was an occasion for laughter. No one had ever heard of the machines and few people at the time were even conscious of the fact that the Japanese were *making* motorcycles. The little men in neat suits walked around the paddock introducing them-selves and taking photographs of everything that moved. 'Excuse me, we from Honda. We take picture. Next year we race.'
Much hilarity.
'Ha ha. Harry Kiri riding the Kami bloody Kazi special.'
Next year they were back, they won no prizes, but the year after that, in 1959 they won the manufacturers' prize and thereafter they were unbeatable. Honda have now withdrawn from motor-

cycle racing to concentrate on motor car racing, leaving the field open for Yamaha, Suzuki, and latterly, Kawasaki. Mike Hailwood, riding a 500cc Honda, still held (in 1974) the track record of 108.8 mph set in 1967.

As Geoff Duke chided me gently when I took his photograph, 'You see, even your camera's Japanese.'

'I warn't even a good beer drinker.'
Mick Grant, works Kawasaki rider

Since I was trained in science and statistics, I have a great suspicion of both. They attempt to describe reality with precision and end by eviscerating it. My statistics will be brief. The Isle of Man circuit is 37.733 miles long; 67 people have lost their lives in T.T. races. This year (1974) a total of 121,528 miles were ridden by competitors in practice and racing. Having disposed of the facts, let us get down to reality.

The Isle of Man circuit is difficult and hence dangerous. There is no denying this. Like some Everest of racing, it is the supreme challenge and on being conquered leads to spiritual highs, which we ordinary men only occasionally emulate with drugs, booze or sex (and I am informed, religion). This high probably accounted for Mick Grant's linguistic confusion.
'I really feel accelerated when I finish. Really!'
'On this bend, you've got to exhilarate just here.'

Because of the intricacies of the circuit, a very powerful solo engine will not now necessarily win the race. In some cases, paradoxically, it might even guarantee that a rider loses. The reason for this is simple. The circuit is not a specially designed banked track where with more power, you can go faster. Because of the number of twists and turns, the full power of the larger bikes can under some conditions (e.g. wet) not be used. The engines, like some barely tame tiger, react badly to this, with snarls and splutters. The circuit is (even though some sections carry the grand title 'A1') a rather ordinary country road. It dips between lanes, passes small villages, winds next to a stream and breathtakingly on top of Snaefell, you can, on a clear day, see Scotland, England, Wales and the

John Williams met this wall very quickly.

mountains of Morne in Ireland. It has been vastly improved since the 'good old days', when it was nothing more than a sheep track. Lately it has been improved year by year. Some corners widened ('making it easy for them' — T.T. veteran) and some stretches smoothed down.
'I just don't like these new stretches. Look slippy to me. Also where the new bits start, that bump at full throttle, you're airborne.' Mick Grant, discussing the resurfaced section on the mountain.

This twisting ribbon of road imposes restrictions on the riders. The first of these is that all the top riders ride at below what they know is their limit, for if they come off here at a hundred and fifty miles an hour, a speed they often surpass, it is unlikely they will come to rest against a straw bale. They are more likely to hit a wall, a tree, a house, a bank. At that speed the human body is a frail thing indeed.

The more powerful bikes pose another problem here. As Mick Grant said,
'Yer see, on a 350 I know I can tek this corner at full noise. On the Kawasaki (a 750cc monster) I just don't know. It's a bit shit or bust.'
The fact of excess speed and power, was reiterated by many riders. 'You see, not too long ago, here you could turn it on full tap and sail round, no problems. The bike could do a hundred and thirty and you could take the corner at *exactly* that speed. But now my bike does a hundred and seventy. If I make a mistake and try that corner at over a hundred and thirty I am going to have problems. Big problems.'
So the corners and bends are the iron laws of circuit, to break them is to flirt with disaster. This is the one reason that Mike Hailwood's record for 500cc, for the circuit has stood for so long even though the motorcycles have improved in power a great deal. (There is also something which is usually glossed over — Hailwood was indisputably a rider of genius and as Geoff Duke said, 'Ago

Chapter 5

was pushing him all the way.')

A number of riders have pronounced on how to take the multitude of corners and bends on the Isle of Man.
'You go up Snaefell on the machine and come down on your nerves.' Bob MacIntyre.
'Go in slow, come out fast.' Geoff Duke.
'Go in under control, come out fast.' **Mike Grant**.
'I don't know, what lies did I tell you last time?' Jack Findlay.
But all agree that you have to know the correct line and hence have an intimate knowledge of every bump and curve, large or small, not only to win, but also to survive.

The meandering road is different to the rider and the spectator. On the straights the spectator sees, what is for the first time, a rather frightening sight, of an impersonal machine, not a man and a machine, hammering past, tearing the air with a high-pitched scream. The man becomes a machine, because he blends intimately with the motorcycle. Adding to this mechanical aspect, is the fact that not an inch of skin is visible, because of racing leathers, boots and gloves and the space-age crash helmets, which totally block from view any human response on the part of the rider. There is no place or time to see a grimace, a flicker of impatience.

Despite the fact that at extremely high speeds the road for the racers narrows alarmingly and the houses on the side crowding disturbingly, they see a great deal. From a line of spectators, astonishingly, at well over a hundred miles an hour, they will recognize someone they know. One asked me, 'Saw you at Highlander trying to get pictures. Did you get one of me?'
He was clocked at over 140 mph. One ex-rider explained,
'I gave up when I couldn't pick out individual spectators — when they all became a blur I knew I was getting past it.'

I went round the circuit in a number of ways, in different vehicles. The first was with the Isle of Man Tourist Board's

Press Officer. He pointed out places of historic interest.
'That house belongs to the Christian family. Fletcher Christian
came from here.'
He omitted to mention that Bligh too, was a Manxman. We had a
leisurely tour, stopping for tea at Ramsay. I was filled with information on the good character of Manxmen and women, and
frowned upon when I took a photograph of a notice on the road
at Brandish (a high speed section) with the words 'Accident Black
Spot'. I was off loaded at the finish and wished well.

The next trip round was on a motorcycle. The acquisition of a
motorcycle was itself a minor miracle. Over the race weeks on the
Island there is an ordered list of availability of life's necessities.
Liquor (easy), women (more difficult), and transport (impossible).
All hireable vehicles on the Island are booked solid from January.
A telephone call was made on my behalf by a pretty secretary at
the Auto Cycle Union office. She telephoned an ex-rider, who is
now a marshall and runs an excellent motorcycle sales and service
shop, Neil Kelly. Could he, as a favour . . . ? Miraculously, he lent
me a bike immediately. Sensing that I had not ridden for some
time (ten years actually) he wished me well and stuffed the bike's
manual in my pocket. I changed instantly from a tired television
producer/writer to a dashing young blade.

A motorcycle in one way renders one vulnerable; there is no
roof or safety belt, but ah, the joy of motorcycle riding! You are
in direct contact with your environment. You smell all the delici-
ous tiny pastoral smells. If it is warm, you are warm and exuberant,
if it is cold and miserable, you are likewise. I did a leisurely tour of
the circuit. My first stop was at the 'Halfway Inn'. The beer had
been recommended to me by a television producer. Whatever else
his faults, his taste in beer is firstclass. I was served by an extremely ancient woman who said nothing while I drank and paid for my
·excellent pint. I started my motorcycle again and drove around
the circuit. The wooded areas had a faint sharp smell, pleasant,
rather like wild onions, not found in England. Overhead, birds

twittered and ahead, cows lowed. Evidence of the race blended
oddly with the countryside. Ticking off the miles was a large blue
sign with a baleful countenance. This was a helmeted and goggled
rider, a symbol of a motorcycling publication which looked like
one of Dr. Who's more dangerous opponents.

The bikers roared past me, almost all of them riding very badly.
At certain corners I began to appreciate some of the talents one
needs to be a very fast rider. Previously I had had some ill-defined
idea that they were a motley group who somehow managed to
push their bikes round the track quickly. Exactly how I did not
know. True enough, one accelerated here, leant there, braked some
other time. It was on the Veranda that I realized there was something else. I took the bend at a breathtaking sixty miles an hour.
The riders double that speed. Besides skill, craftsmanship, flair, call
it what you will, there is another ingredient — courage. Sheer raw
nerve to dominate road and machine. This is seldom thought about
and never discussed. On the road there were occasional gaps,
punched in the dry stone walls, not only momentoes of man's
folly, but also tributes to his courage.
'Here the bike's leapin' all over the place, wheels three foot off the
floor, handlbars slappin' lock to lock. The machine's unbelievable.
Everythin' becomes intuitive.'
And the intuition is dominated by courage.

The old saying, 'Any fool can drive straight, it's the corners that
separate the men from the boys,' is nowadays not quite correct.
The top factory machines can do 170 mph on the very short
straights on the Island. The problem experienced by a number of
riders — Findlay, Smart, Grant et al, is simply of keeping the bike
in a straight line.
'The cross wind between the houses knocks you about,' said one.
'It's not the corners, that's instinct you know. Where to poke it in,
where to crank it . . . .' Then Findlay smiled in puzzlement,
'but at Sulby Straight, you get problems *there*.'
Mick Grant agreed. 'I have to knock it off on the Kawasaki to

keep it under control.'
Sulby has another characteristic, being the straight on the lowest
part of the course, makes it the place where the bike is most likely
to seize or experience mechanical failure. It also speaks volumes
for the state of the fine art of carburation, that a difference in alti-
tude can seize a bike if it is not correct.

All the riders I spoke to had fallen off on the Isle of Man, either
in practice or in a race, but the top riders only injure themselves
by act of God. Their skill is such that they are able to control to
an astonishing degree any mistake *they* make.
'Well I had the choice of sliding it or hitting a bale so I hit the bale,
reckoned I'd do less damage to the bike.' Grant after colliding at
Creg-ny-Baa and then coming second in the Lightweight race.
'I put it in a slide and the copper was so certain I was going to lose
it and hit him, he ran away.' Findlay in Senior T.T. race. But it is
the unexpected, a mechanical failure that causes almost all the
serious accidents among the best riders. By and large they were
philosophical about such accidents, over which they had little or
no control.
'No use worryin' about it. All it does is meks you go slower.' Grant.
'Well not much you can do. I don't think about it.' Smart.
'I don't think about it at all, it's bad psychology.' Findlay.
This stoicism in the face of danger, combined with their enjoyment
of speed, led me to question some of the riders in depth. The
results were personal portraits which were in some respects as fasci-
nating as the races themselves.

Like the machines they ride the solo racers displayed some characteristics in common. A journalist informed me drunkenly one night
that one similarity was that *all* rider took drugs before *any* important race. This displayed a depth of ignorance about the racers
probably only equalled by the mendacity of the popular news-
paper for which he worked. Not only do they *not* take drugs, they
drink little or nothing. Findlay however did confess that he was
partial to whiskey.

Chapter 5

'How much?'
'One tot a week.'
He smiled as though he had stumbled on a new philosophy of life.

All of the solo riders are small men physically, or if tall are athletically thin. My six foot four bulk towered above all of them. Doug Lunn, a tiny man riding a huge Ducati, insisted that physical strength and bulk were not necessary for a rider. On a side car you do however need strong arms.

The other characteristic which they share, is that the best riders definitely have the best looking women. They are easy to remember. Charlie Williams' girlfriend Anne, blonde and beautiful with a radiant smile, was timing Charlie when I spoke to her. Did she get worried for Charlie? She smiled at me with dazzling incomprehension.
'Of course not, Charlie's such a good rider.'
Mick Grant's girlfriend Carol, or as she rather tartly informed me, fiancée, red-haired like Mick, was elegantly unimpressed by all the ballyhoo going on when Mick won.

Jack Findlay introduced me to his wife Nanou, an urbane and infinitely interesting Parisienne, who went on to inform me,
'Pah . . . we are not married . . . we are, 'ow you say, friends.'
Almost all the riders were courteous to the various camp followers they attracted. Whenever I spoke to Findlay we would be loudly interrupted by Australians.
'Hi there Jack. Howzit going? Jack, I want you to meet the little woman, Beth. Beth, say hello to Jack. Jeezus Jack, it's been how many years now? How you doing?'
Jack would smile, shake hands and I would try to remember what we had been talking about only to be interrupted again.
'Say you there, do me and Jack a favour. Press the tit on the little black box, and now one with Beth as well. Smile Beth.'
I would duly record smiles all round and then scowl at the intruders.

Jack was brought up in a small town near (in Australian terms) Melbourne. He hated school.

'Sometimes I could barely sit still I wanted to get outside so badly.' He always wanted to do only one thing — race motorcycles. He started riding, illegally, aged twelve and entered races when he was under age, a fact he is still guilty about today.

'You won't tell anyone will you?' he pleaded appealingly.

Of all the riders, in style he most resembles Geoffrey Duke.

'I aim . . . my idea of perfection, is not to hang off the machine like some riders, but to be part of it. And then try and go very fast.' And how did he go very fast?

'For this you need the correct line, you get this from experience, not watching for the third dustbin on the left and all that, plus a certain gift for geometry, angles and curves and studying the female figure.'

Since he also quoted his religion as being sex, he obviously enjoys his work. He confirmed this more seriously.

'I'm one of those people who is very lucky. I enjoy doing what I'm doing. I wouldn't do anything else.'

When I saw him come hammering towards me at well over 150 mph, his bike seeming to make for a cottage wall and certain disaster, I was not too sure. Then he did the impossible and quite deliberately missed annihilation by an inch. I remembered back to his quiet confidence and trust in himself.

'I've always been a bit shy and that's a drawback, but I believed if I was good enough I would make it without, you know, a lot of rubbish. This winter's the first time I'll be able to relax, keep fit and not have to work to save money to fix my motorcycles. It's never happened before.'

He also spoke with quiet simplicity about how he brought his mother over from Australia to show her what he did.

'I reckon I did her proud — and she was proud of me too.'

He was preparing himself for a race the next day.

'I need to be quiet, on my own, you know,' he said a little

apologetically. 'I've got to ride well, they don't pay me £1000 to watch the scenery.'
And were he to win?
'Then I start planning the next race. I know it sounds a bit disappointing but memories are things to live with when you get old.'

Jack Findlay's team mate Paul Smart is the one man whose face is not criss-crossed by the big and small scars that most motorcycle racers have.
'I was the first to discover the Bell Star crash helmet.'
Like Findlay, he disliked school — 'Worst years of my life.'
After school he drifted from job to job.
'My old man got me a job in a photographic agency — photography was his hobby. I guess he reckoned I'd nick enough stuff to keep his hobby going.'
From there he went to sea and on to an apprenticeship in ship-building. It was during this period that he started racing.
'The first five years were terrible, short of cash, bad machines, coming nowhere in races. Then I started to get better.'
On his own admission, Smart is a ragged, untidy rider. But he is also, undeniably, a very fast rider.
'You've got to concentrate. If you're not concentrating you're not going fast enough.'

When I spoke to him he had just flown in from the United States and was understandably tired. On top of this his works motorcycles were giving trouble. The weather worried him.
'I cant stand racing in the wet. Once I was doing 140 mph and I started aquaplaning. My bike slowly turned round,' he picked up a spanner and expressionlessly turned it around in illustration, 'so there I was doing 140 mph, backwards! And there was nothing I could do. Absolutely nothing.'
He came out of the crash in one piece. His ambition?
'To become a team manager, then I'll withdraw my riders from the International Grand Prixs. Do you know, they have audiences in

'I wont eat of this plate'

the hundred thousands and the prize money is sometimes round a
hundred quid. Someone's getting stinking bloody rich off us.'
How did he feel about himself now?
'Well you only get to be a works rider if you are good and being a
professional rider is a bit like being chosen as President of a
country.'
He went over to listen to his motorcycle.

Mike Grant is a Yorkshireman, probably one of the few I have
ever met whose accent is a delight to listen to.
'Oh I was average at school, but I tried more or less everythin',
even drinkin' beer, but I warn't even a very good beer drinker, then
at Art College I started racin'. Hello, I thought, I can mek somethin'
out o' this. Well I stopped drinkin' beer, lost two stone and I seem
to be mekkin' out alright now.'

In two weeks Mick picked up about two thousand pounds in
prize and start money. On top of this he would have received additional monies from sponsors (Shellsport, Reynolds chains) and an
additional inducement from the Auto Cycle Union.

John Williams had mentioned getting his juices right before a
race. Mick was more explicit.
'Everything depends on mental attitude. I have to be in the right
frame of mind before a race. Aggressive, but not too aggressive
mind. Just so's you don't do nothin' daft.'

Of all the riders, Mick took infinite pains to initiate me into the
mysteries of riding hard and fast. I owe him a profound debt, not
only for that, but also for his patience.
'No, me name's Mick Grant, not Williams.' (This after I had been
seeing him every day for a week.)

Besides the craft and courage needed to push the bikes very fast
round the Isle of Man circuit, a certain amount of race strategy is
needed. On a short circuit where all the riders start together, a

rider has to jockey for leadership of the pack. Then he can do a variety of things to impede his rivals. Such tactics on the Isle of Man are useless. Since the riders start in pairs at timed intervals, what a rider is doing, is racing the clock, not necessarily the man ahead of him. The man ahead of him may not be ahead in race position, similarly, for the man behind. Mechanics and timekeeper/ friends placed at strategic points on the circuit signal the racer's position.

'I get behind a man and after two or three bends I can tell where I can take him. Everyone's got a characteristic style. So I work it out an' I know, ah yes, he'll be a bit slow at Greeba, and I know what his line will be, so I tek him there.' Mick Grant.

'Also I watch when he passes a tree say, then I count until I pass the tree and if I estimate the distance I can work out the speed and how many seconds behind him I am.'

Elementary calculations, try them some day, winding in and out of corners at 130 mph. On top of this Mick had his right hand encased in plaster. I made a lazy mental note of this. Only much later was I told the proper implications.

I asked him how he viewed his style.

'Well I get lazy, but I cover up by ridin' fast.'

We drove past Brandish, a very fast corner where I had photograph-ed the 'Accident Black Spot' sign.

'It's right comical here,' said Mick. 'On race day there's a line of black boots sat on the wall there, an' if I'm going real fast all the boots tip over backwards, out of the way, they get that scared.'

During one race when Mick was going 'real fast' I watched at Brandish for a while. Exactly as predicted, as he threw himself with relish into the corner, the spectators, like macabre black-booted Tiller girls, flung themselves backwards in unison, off the wall. I smiled a little smile of secret knowledge.

On most bends Mick was happy.

'When you do it proper you and the bike feel good.'

One such corner for him is Cronk-ny-Mona.

Chapter 5

'It's verra good fer spectating. You get behind the bank on the left hand side of the road and you're just about level with the rider's eyes. An' the rider's cranked over an' all he can see is the sky. I keep the power on until the arrer — actually I keep it on quite a bit further than that, but I tell everyone that, then they brake early.'
So rivals, now you know.

The sidecar riders, when I could pry them out from underneath their machines, were always helpful. There was an air of grumbling happiness about all of them, an absence of tension, which the solo riders did not share. A few spoke of the man who had been killed on the first day of practice with quiet dispassion, then there would be a pause and they would pass on to other topics, mainly their 'chairs'. Inside the area where almost all the sidecar combination riders were camped, I spoke to them. Mick Wortley explained in great detail the design geometry of his combination which he had built from scratch. The handling characteristics of a combination depend on this initial design. Then there are the fine details. 'Look where I stuck the battery, that's saved space. Good i'n't it?'
The race.
'Well, I can't stand watching. I always wish I were out there.'

A gloomy Alan Sansum appeared.
'What's the matter?'
'The engine's missing and I've stripped it and put it together and the bloody thing's still missing. I don't know.'
He ran his fingers through his curly black hair. He was one of the few riders who had a sponsor, Rod Quaife. Rod looked at the offending machine, his eyes also gloomy.
'Give it a rest. Tomorrow we'll change the carb slides.'
But they started the engine again and Alan roared up the road. At peak revs there was a just perceptible misfire. He came back, stopped and in despair, looked at the engine. His son pedalled around furiously on a toy motorcycle.
'Sod it,' said Alan, disappearing into his tent.

Fred and Les Lewin are unusual in that they are a husband and wife team. People would drift in and out of their Transit, borrowing a gear, asking for help. It was always graciously given, Fred usually excusing himself then returning, smiling, to the conversation. Les met Fred through her brother.

'Well, you know what's it's like. You're supposed to meet prospectives through your brother. Well I looked at the friends he had and I've never met a scruffier lot of greasers in my life, really!' Lesley's middle-class accent (which she occasionally forgets to suppress) was more pronounced at the memory. 'Well then one day Fred came around and we went to Brands and he borrowed a combination and asked me whether I'd like to have a go. Nothing fast. So the first lap he went around slowly, then a little bit faster then he said lean here, move there, and all that, and on lap ten I was jumping up and down. Come on, come on, let's get really moving!' Les clenched her fists and blushed faintly.

'That's how it started.'

She was then aged sixteen. Their engine?

'Well Ron, I'm British, an' I'm proud of it I suppose. I know our engines could be better. But it's best to use them and they'll get better — you see,' Fred grinned embarrassedly and pulled at his short spiky hair, 'it's no use using the other engines. It's not a motorboat after all, is it?'

Fred had an easygoing attitude towards the race.

Nervous Naa not me, she is though.'

'I get so tense I can't speak. I feel terrible. It's all bottled up inside me, then when we go, whaam!'

The sentiments seemed strange at first to me, coming as they did from a woman who had about her an air of beautiful solidity. As an ex-international swimmer, I suppose the competitiveness has become part of her nature.

'An' she's a good mechanic, timin' an' all an' not too bad with the brazing torch,' said Fred.

They brought her mother to watch them one year. She was too terrified to watch the race and sat in the tent all day. Les, with

some scientific precision (she is a scientist when she is not racing)
explained to me what one does as the passenger in a sidecar.
'The point is not to fight gravity but to balance it. That way you
don't need much strength. But anyway it is mostly the driver.'
Fred scowled and pulled on his hair.
'Aah now, that's not true Ron . . . . '
How did Fred ride then?
'Well I go a little more careful than when I was a young 'un,
specially with Les now. You know with us, it's a sport, not a livin',
we have our jobs.'
'Besides you don't walk away from an accident here,' said Les.
Since Lesley was such a good mechanic and so on, who did the
cooking?
Lesley turned red.
'Ah well . . .' said Fred. 'If there's a machine to be fixed up we fix
the machine and eat afterwards . . . .'
'Last year we worked two days and nights without eating, remember?' said Lesley.
A fellow rider drifted by to borrow a gearbox off their 'Puddin'
engine', a reserve all-purpose power unit. At the far end of the
camp someone started up a solo. The high-pitched scream was
totally unlike that of the sidecar power units. The two-stroke solos
give out a noise which bites into your ears, a high pitched protest.
The sidecars, almost all powered by four-stroke engines, using
megaphone exhaust systems, emit a deeper note. To me it was
more exciting, vibrating my chest and stomach with its power. The
solos are intellectual, the sidecars visceral.

Gradually, as we waited for the night to arrive, the engine noises
and the screaming seagulls quietened. Douglas settled down, preparing for the morning, when it would be full of the sound of speed
and sights of the sea.

Geoff Duke — the master

Spectators — Young and beautiful .... ▲

.... and not so young ▼

▼ Receding into the mist like mechanical soldiers

'Bloody flies' said Mick ▼

▼ Spectator at Creg-ny-Baa

▲ Trusty gravity fillers — from way back

He died for the sport he loved

◀ Douglas has other things
besides motor bikes

Up, up and away

▼ Silent paddock before a race

Getting ready ▼

▼ Start of 250cc race

10 seconds to the start of Junior TT ▼

▲ With all that expertise scrutineers check the bikes

Scrutineering Nick and Gerry's chair ▲

▲ Rider and wife — early one morning

4 am in the paddock before practice ▲

Beneath the leafy bough they roar and race ▼

▲ Smart wreathed by smoke in the early morning

▼ Looking back from the Guthrie's Memorial

Schons chases Wortley

Dennis and Royston Keen in action ▲

▲ Right — left — right

American entrant Joe and Alma Rochelau ▼

▲ Typical custom built chair
▼ The talk is of engines, engines and engines

▲ Honda being tuned

For sale: Yahama good runner ▲

▲ Down every alleyway somebody is working
▼ Fixing seized Konig

Alan Sansum really getting down to it ▲
Mad sunday — Creg-ny-Baa ▼

Jack Findlay chatting with team manager

Billy McCosh — the old master ▲

▲ Findlay on the clinical Gulf sponsored Norton

Charlie Williams — gentleman of the track ▲

▼ Mick Grant winning 1975 Senior TT

▲ Le Mans start for the 1974 Open Road Race

Chris Revett on Honda CB500 ▲

▲ 1974 Mick Grant, victor on Slippery Sam

▼ Green 'meany' works 750cc Kawasaki

The Rutter/Murray CB400F ▲

Chapter 6

'They couldn't organize a piss-up in a brewery.'
Disgruntled rider

The main organizers of the Isle of Man T.T. races are the Auto Cycle Union (A.C.U.) for whom the race is one event, (albeit the main) in a crowded calendar. The A.C.U. during the race period, is the highly visible tip of an iceberg. They decide on start money for the stars, expenses for the riders, screen the applicants, selecting only the most able and on the Island, sort out, and sometimes inevitably, create problems. Interpretation of the rules is referred to the Stewards' Committee of the A.C.U. What often seems a high-handed or arbitrary ruling, is invariably a carefully considered decision.

A sidecar rider and his partner were on the receiving end of an adverse decision regarding racing a different combination. I was treated to a Byzantine explanation of why the decision had gone against them.
'Well, you see it's our sponsor, he organizes other races and they run perfectly, not like this.'
He swept his arm around disparagingly.

As he laid out his case he became dazzled by the iniquity of the A.C.U., contrasting as it did with his own innocence.
'You know Ron, I get so mad just thinking about it, I almost hit him you know. Jesus, they are so bad they couldn't organize a piss-up in a brewery. Now why couldn't they . . . .'

I heard a number of grouses directed at the A.C.U. and in the end they all boiled down not to incompetence, but to a marked failure in communicating adequately with all parties concerned.

Chapter 6

Vernon Cooper, Chairman of the T.T. Organizing Committee, agreed. 'You must realize that most of our help comes from a lot of dedicated amateurs and mistakes are sometimes made. But I *am* concerned with streamlining the structure.'
Vernon Cooper agreed that there was a curious reluctance on the part of the A.C.U. to publicize itself and this, its last great road race.
'We are our own worst enemies.'
We were interrupted in the middle of our talk by a crusty old ex-T.T. rider.
'Couldn't help overhearing you. Who are you?'
'Vernon Cooper.'
'And what do you do?'
'I'm chairman of the A.C.U.'
'Humph, I must say, never heard of you. Do you come to our annual dinners?'
Cooper blinked. 'Well, I go to a lot of dinners . . . .'

Vernon Cooper is a self-made Northern businessman, passionately interested in racing and takes upon himself the main responsibility for the T.T. races. For this honour he is out of pocket at the end of the races (like most participants) and has had the dubious distinction of sitting on the stage at the prize giving, with a number of other dignitaries, who, in white tie and tails, look rather like a lot of stunned penguins.

The T.T. may soon be downgraded from the world championship, which will of course detract from its status. The reason for the loss of international championship point status, was explained to me by Vernon Cooper.
'Well, it's difficult you see. Say now another country demands that the world championship be held there and they've got a track especially built, then we would have trouble defending the Isle of Man.'
'Which country?'
'Well, the U.S.S.R. for instance.'

Reds under the race track as well.

The twelve 'World Championship' races are held in various tracks in Europe. None is held in the U.S.A., a point brought up by Paul Smart.
'The world championship is meaningless. Gene Romeo came over from the States and cleaned up all the so-called world champions.'
'On the Island as well?'
'Well, no, not here,' he conceded reluctantly.

In straight mechanical terms this race is the equivalent of half a season's racing. Some manufacturers are reluctant to burn out their thoroughbred engines on this one race. With adequate publicity this reluctance to race here could certainly be reversed. What was once the world's most important race could become so again. A situation could be created where to ignore the race of races on the Isle of Man, would be construed as a sign of mediocrity and hence failure.

The degree of sheer organization needed for the race can be judged from the fact that the day after the last race was run, the first meeting was convened to discuss the next year's races.

Besides organizing the riders and races, the A.C.U. liaises with a number of bodies: the F.I.M. (world body for championship motorcycle rules and races), the Manx authorities, the police, medical help, the Tourist Board on the Isle of Man, the press, radio and so on.

Just before the races an assorted group of journalists was waiting in front of the press office for accreditation, information and all the plethora of rubbish which goes to make news. The press officer was late; in the drizzle there were mutterings of discontent. At last the press officer arrived and we all crowded damply into the Nissen hut that was the press office. The official looked us over with distaste.

'I see it's the usual bunch. Never met a bigger lot of scroungers in
my life.'
The gentlemen of the press looked at him coldly. War, I felt, was
definitely being declared.

As Vernon Cooper said, 'We are our own worst . . . .'

Viewing the race, or 'spectating' as they so horribly call it, costs
nothing, except for a few specially built stands and a few free enterprise Manxmen who rent out seats in their gardens. The race for
the A.C.U. is expensive. The money, not enough, comes from
various sources, but primarily from the Isle of Man Tourist Board.
They are not lavish, but they know a good thing when they see it,
especially in the guise of some thirty thousand tourists over two
weeks. The amount they give varies, depending on whom one talks
to, but it is in the region of eighty thousand pounds. It disappears
with consummate ease into the race.

Getting the people there and back is the business of the Isle of
Man Steam Packet Company. They, to quote a manager, 'Give a
substantial amount to the T.T. races'. Last year (1973) their nett
profit was just under £500,000. They contributed £1,000 to the
races. Perhaps it is contradictions like this which led the above
manager to forbid me to record our conversation.
'Because the B.B.C. have done it before and they misquoted me.'
Fortunately I have an excellent memory (and a remote switch on
my tape recorder).

At the same session I was lectured on the virtues of free enterprise (I.o.M.S.P.C. have a monopoly), profits ('Don't see why it
should be a dirty word') and finally how no shareholders made any
money out of the Isle of Man Steam Packet Company. Their
Annual General Meeting seems redolent with comic possibilities.

Considering that it costs the average rider a great deal to bring
over his machine, van, mechanic etc. etc., a generous reduction in

fares to these people by the Steam Packet Company would be both a practical and a handsome gesture.

Another unique institution which has become closely identified with the race is Manx Radio. Over race weeks their broadcasts are models of acutely informed observation, equalling if not bettering the B.B.C. coverage of old. (Nowadays the B.B.C. has lost its former enthusiasm.) There are commentators around the track at regular intervals and a few with soft Irish brogues, in an odd way complimenting the skill of the riders and the difficulty of the race. The commentators' skill was almost mandatory, because of the number of highly informed spectators, who would pounce with dedicated delight on any slight mistake. The non-race broadcasts were also enchanting. Where else would a Beethoven symphony be interrupted to extol the virtues of a soap powder? The results of this juxtaposition of Square Deal Surf, with Ludwig von Beethoven intellectually and musically are indescribable. What was interesting was the fact that Beethoven *was* being broadcast, in the face of Garry Glitter and the rest of the musical giants. Then the messages. 'John X is looking for two Honda 250, 7S, carbs., can anyone help?'
The news bulletins were equally interesting.
'The proposed irrigation scheme, 26 acres in Onchan, is to go ahead as scheduled. The Isle of Man Steam Packet Company is offering reduced fares in September. This offer will not hold on Mondays, Tuesdays, Wednesdays . . . . . It is hoped that this scheme will greatly encourage tourism in the slack season. Those are the news headlines. Now for the local news. Yesterday in Peel, a dog . . . .'
Nixon was at the time fighting his last deluded fight against the media and assorted lawmen. Still, I suppose on balance, history may prove Manx Radio correct in ignoring him.

Equally part of the race is the Manx Police Force. The large, burly policemen are presided over by a short, genial man 'A real copper at last' as one policeman informed me. Chief Superintendent Weedon, head of the leviathans, told me that he was 'The most

important man . . . ah policeman here'. The police, over the holi-
The police, over the holiday period, have a number of problems,
chief amongst them being that some one hundred and ten men and
women have to look after hundreds and thousands of hoi polloi.
In the end it boils down to the police getting too little sleep, which
may account of the slightly acid response I got when I was taking
photographs at the start of the race.
'Come on now, get back there, on to the pavement.'
'If you ask him (a photographer in front of me) to get back, then
we'll all be able to see,' I said reasonably.
The young policeman turned round red in the face and in a most
uncopperly fashion said, 'And why don't you mind your own
bloody business.'
The more experienced men take the race and the long hours in
their stride, as one said to me, 'This is physical, it's easy, but the
fight against crime, that takes it out of you, *that's* physical and
mental.'
Another policeman with some twenty-six years of service, had definite ideas about the riders.
'They're the most selfish people I've ever met. I've scraped more
than I care to remember off the road and I'll tell you what they
always ask, a) How's my bike? b) Can I have a cigarette? c) Let my
pit know and d) Let my folks know. Now I ask you, isn't that
selfish?'
He went on to tell me how he saw a German crash with his sidecar.
'Well, he kicked the thing straight, swearing twelve to the dozen in
Kraut, then he pushed the self starter but the bike was still in gear
and with him standing there it takes off and hits the nearest wall.
Well, you should have seen and heard that lot.'
The rider eventually remounted and rode on.

To me, all of this was not an illustration of the rider's selfishness
but the tension involved in the race and the total dedication almost
all of them have to racing. This zeal sometimes conflicts with offic-
ialdom. Nowhere is this more obvious than inside the scrutineers'
tent. This is where the bikes are passed prior to setting out on the

track. The scrutineers are usually ex-riders or engineers or both. In amongst all the tension, with the riders' nervous desire to get out on the track, the scrutineers' single-mindedness in seeing that the bikes are roadworthy sometimes results in upset.

I watched them checking a number of bikes. Tink, tink, Les Griffiths, chief scrutineer, tapped the spokes with a large nail.
'Just to see they're all O.K.'
He tugged on cables and pipes.
'Hello, what's this then?'
A pipe came away.
'Must have another clip on it.'
'Do it when I come back.'
'No, before you go out.'
'Bloody hell, that pipe will never . . . .'
'Before.'
The rider sent a message to his mechanic. When the offending pipe was secure a little star was pasted on his cowling and he left. A few bikes later,
'This is not good enough.'
The front brake cable had come adrift with a tug. The rider glared at the scrutineer.
'Come on now lad, you know if this comes off, you've no brakes and it's tickets.'
The bike was pushed back to the mechanic. The scrutineer turned to me.
'We try and see that the bikes are as safe as possible, brakes, pipes and a couple of little things that we know about, or rather what we know will happen, after a couple of laps here.'
Another competitor, a German, appeared. The scrutineer spoke slowly to him.
'Washer, need washer here. Other bike yesterday. Crash! No washer! You get?'
The German went to get a washer for a rear suspension.
'On the circuit here there's more wear and tear you see,' he explained. After the solos had been inspected and passed, the side-

car combinations appeared.

'They're the real headache. You'll never believe the tricks these boys get up to. Some are positively lethal. Yesterday I had one with practically no brakes. You know what he said? "I'll drift it round corners". Drift it!' His voice rose in indignation.

He disappeared under an oily array of pipes to check whether a sidecar frame was sound.

'O.K. Bill, slap a star on this one.'

'Right ho.'

They worked hard, unloved and unsung.

In the event of a serious accident however, the medical organization on the Island is probably among the best, if not *the* best in the world. There is a well-equipped and staffed hospital, but equally important there is a helicopter on stand-by to get the casualties to hospital quickly and efficiently. The medical services come under Dr. Pat Cullen, a young doctor who organizes the services at his disposal with considerable skill. He talked to me while a practice was going on, about what happens in medical terms when the human body travelling very fast, hits an immovable object.

'Massive rupture, sometimes they are literally split down the middle. But those are few and far between. Mostly there is rupture of some internal organ or organs. Spleen, aorta, liver, the thing here is to diagnose and operate as quickly as possible.'

('You can tell after a while those that have had it, they go a sort of grey.' Helicopter pilot)

Dr Cullen had taken the incident book, a book containing a description of all accidents in all races and analysed where the points of maximum danger were.

'Undoubtedly the stretch between Ballacraine and Kirk Michael. Before that the accidents are usually minor, at low speed at Quarter Bridge for instance . . . .'

At that precise moment someone came running in.

'Accident at Quarter Bridge, can you see him?'

'Excuse me,' said Dr. Cullen and walked into the corridor. Standing there was Charlie Williams, a little red in the face. He looked at his feet.

'I came off.'

'Anything broken?'

One of his arms was already in a plaster cast, a momento from another race.

'I don't know, hurt my hand a bit.'

Then remembering that he might be forbidden to race with two broken arms he amended this.

'I mean, is this alright?' and held out his arm.

He was an almost perfect illustration of what the policeman had mistakenly called selfishness. He had been geared up to ride, had ridden too fast and come off. Now he was experiencing a counter tension, not a well-it's-all-over-now deflation, but a visible willing of his body to stop shaking, to appear calm, when every nerve was screaming for release.

Dr. Cullen examined his hand.

'Open . . . . shut . . . . any pain?'

'No.'

'And here?'

'No.'

'That's alright then.'

The question tumbled out.

'Can I carry on riding?'

'Of course.'

Then his hand started shaking. He left to get on to another motorcycle.

'Almost perfect illustration of a Quarter Bridge accident,' said Dr. Cullen. We spoke of some of the more serious accidents. Talking about death in strictly medical terms I was aware how it became a cleaner end, not the dirty messy business that it actually is.

'The doctor had his hand down the fella's throat, trying to fish out the bits of false teeth that were choking him to death.' Witness to accident.

Despite the efficiency of the medical services there is a limit to what can be done.

'There is no preventative medicine — one cannot innoculate against accidents,' said Dr. Cullen.

How did he personally view the riders, some of whom would depend for their lives on his care?

'I don't think they are fools, some are brave, some are a little lacking in imagination,' he paused. 'I think one can say that they do not regard life as something which should be held on to terribly dearly.'

Chapter 7

'Yer doin' it wrong.'
Billie McCosh

Official practices start a week ahead of the actual races. On the first day of practise a man was killed. Peter Lingard Hardy. He was riding a sidecar combination with his twin brother as passenger. The sidecar riders and passengers, usually garrulous to a fault, spoke only a little about the accident.
'He was very experienced. Something must have happened that he couldn't control.'
And less charitably,
'Well I don't know Ron, I said when I saw him, there's an accident looking for a place to happen.'

I later discovered that my initial thoughts on reading of Hardy's death on the top of the Grandstand had been correct. Using all the skill that he possessed, he had tried to steer his skidding combination through the only gap available, between two, solid, stone gateposts. He almost made it, he saved his twin brother, another six inches and he too would have been safe.

Cause of death? A throttle cable snapped, just as he was putting the power on in a corner. The high compression engine, throttle closed, locked the back wheel, which started the skid. He could, I suppose, have rolled off the machine, hoped for the best, and left his brother to fend for himself. But he chose to do what he courageously knew best. He locked on the front brake and aimed with his life for the small gap in the stone wall.

It was with an understandable despondency that practices got under way. In the welter of sound, determination and excitement, present reality soon overtook a past death.

Chapter 7

Every rider approaches practice differently. Some discuss their difficulties with others, some like Geoff Duke, are loners.
'I once tried to talk to other riders about problems on some of the corners, but it was useless. So I went back to doing it on my own again.' Jack Findlay.
His friend Nanou, 'When I first saw the track I was terrified. But then I see you must know it.' She lit a cigarette and inhaled deeply. 'And there is one thing. Jack, he is the man with his 'and on the throttle. No-one else. He makes it go slow or faster, it is up to him only.'
Findlay goes out only on practice days on his race machine.
'All those other blokes that go around on road bikes before practice. Well, it maybe O.K. for them, but for me, the right line maybe on the right hand side of the road. You can't get there with traffic coming at you. Also there's a difference taking a corner at forty and a hundred and forty. No, all it does is confuse me. I stick to the proper machines and proper practices.'

The riders, highly skilled though they may be on circuits, if this is their first time on the Island, usually find it useful to tour the circuit and inspect the hundred and twenty kinks and bends with a more experienced rider. This, however, also carries dangers.
'When I first coom 'ere, at Mayhill an experienced rider told me, "Peel off 'ere at the beginnin' of the black' an' white markers", so I did and I war in serious difficulty. Me mate he coom off badly. See the right line for one man is not necessarily the same for another.' Mick Grant.
But Mick also admitted that doing a lap together with Peter Williams, who knows the circuit initmately and gave unstintingly of his knowledge, pushed his lap time up from 100 mph to 105 mph on the next time around. There are a number of obligatory laps which the novice must complete before he will be allowed to race. A very experienced rider can in exceptional circumstance have this rule wholly or partially waived, but it is rare. For the rider who does not know the Isle of Man, the track presents formidable obstacles.

If there is a corner, on your daily route to and from work, with clear visibility (and perhaps no speed traps) try, over a period of time, to discover what the *safe* limit is for taking this one bend. Remember when you go into the bend to use the whole road, remember to be in the correct gear, remember to be at peak revs, remember to accelerate at the correct point on the bend, remember to leave yourself an imperceptible leeway to cope with the unexpected, remember . . . . the list is endless. If you are an exceptionally gifted rider or driver, the chances are that you will take that one corner at about three quarters the speed which an experienced rider would do, using *your* machine. That is just one corner. If you have a multitude of corners and you have more power than you can sensibly use, power that chops its way in instantly with a giant punch, you can see why practices are vital.

Practice used to be carried out with normal traffic (or the more imprudent) out on the road. With increased speeds, the number of practice fatalities increased dramatically, until roads were officially closed during practice times. To minimise inconvenience to the public, some practices start at 5 a.m. This necessitates the riders and mechanics being up by about 4 a.m. to get their bikes and combinations through the scrutineers on time. For everyone, early morning practices are the equivalent of early Mass to Catholics. Only the very devout and insane attend.

I, to my own surprise, woke up at about three in the morning and slipped out of my hotel like a thief. All of Douglas seemed asleep. I went to the camping area reserved for participants and everyone was asleep except a methodical Swiss shaving himself carefully. The camp awoke slowly. Silently the sky changed from purple, to an incandescent pink cloud-streaked vista, that had an aching beauty about it. I wondered whether on this morning there would be someone for whom this would be the last, most lovely sunrise.

Chapter 7

The first motorcycle was an intruder on the silence. It coughed apologetically to a halt but then another motor started. In the scrutineers' tent, in a light made yellow by the sunrise, machines were being examined.

'Been up for some time, must be ready for the riders,' observed one.

'Don't you get tired?'

There was to be another practice that evening, which meant two days of waking before three in the morning and finishing after nine at night. When they got to bed I did not know.

'No, you don't get too tired — besides we enjoy it,' said Les Griffiths.

In the cold morning air, the exhaust gases of the machines were condensing into billowing clouds. Above pink striations in the sky, below sounds and scenes from the inferno, as the gases swirled and enveloped their makers.

Before practice, the riders stand tensely waiting for the winking light, which means nothing to the spectator but signals the beginning of a dangerous learning for the rider. The scream of engines hurts the ears at close quarters.

'Yes it's quite interesting. One of the doctors has made a study of the noise and the Suzuki will actually damage your hearing if you stand behind them too long.' Dr. Pat Cullen.

The sound is a sensation closely akin to having a wasp crawl inside your ear and sting you. The riders fortunately, race away from the sound. Winking light and two more riders are away. Two move up ready, wink and away.

'In the early mornin' you've got problems 'ere. The sun's on yer side ye see. Then you turn an' that Shell garage an' sign blocks out the sun and suddenly it hits you right in the eyes. Can't see nothin' for two or three seconds. Lots of young uns coom off here.' Mick Grant on the sweeping corner at Kirk Michael.

Another problem in the morning is birds. A number of riders

came back with the feathered remnants of pigeons plastered on their farings, disproving the old adage.

On practice the newcomers have to learn not only the bends, the minute characteristics of the road ('See that little lump there, if you change at nine thousand and give it the gun, you'll take off — forever.') and their machines handling characteristics, but most important, the sequence of bends.
'You have to think ahead, how fast do I need to be when I get into the next bend and the next and the next.'
The more experienced strive for the unattainable — perfection.
'Well, if I can coom out of one bend at eight and a half I try to do it at nine the next. But there is a limit you know . . . .' Mick Grant.
Mick also explained why the corners were so important.
'If I can coom out five mile an hour faster, I've still got five mile an hour on the other bloke four hundred yards up the road. That's about two, three seconds. Multiply that by a hundred and twenty bends and you can see how to win the race.'
There is an additional problem for the fast experienced riders, the slow, inexperienced (in Isle of Man terms) riders.
'Well, I came around at about hundred and thirty and there was some bugger in the middle of the road doing about sixty. It's not good enough, they'll have to do something about it.' Jack Findlay on a 750cc Suzuki, complaining about a novice 125cc rider.
Down in the paddock most of the solos were away and I noticed an immaculate sidecar outfit. ('Customized' as the owner later confided to me.) Near it, were what on first sight appeared to be Jack Sprat and his wife. Tall lean Joe Rochelau, from America, was standing next to his short plum ('It's only winter fat.') but still attractive passenger/wife. How did she feel?
'Ohboy, ohboy, ohboy, real nervous!'

After the practice they discovered that their frame of their combination had five hairline cracks in it. Welding started.
'Well, it cost us about $3,000 to get ourselves and the sidecar out here. We regard it as a sort of exciting but expensive vacation.'

They live in the Mid-West of the U.S.A., Michigan. Joe works for
General Motors, Alma in a mail order firm. For them the Island
was different from all else in their lives.
'Wow, this is a real hard track to learn, not like the short circuits
back home.'
'I get the feeling the men don't really like me. They think it's a
man's sport. You have a more male dominated society than we
have. When we pass them, I get some real mean looks . . . .'
There was an eloquent silence, then their mechanic, plump, affable
Ron Silverberg spoke up,
'Well, they may have a point. I mean in a crisis situation, an eye-
lash away from disaster, a woman is more likely to panic . . . .'
His girlfriend, a long-legged bait of a blonde, regarded us all in
silence and I suspect, with a little contempt.
Alma explained her riding style to me.
'I lean out, till I can just feel my backside touching the road, then
I know I'm about right.'
At a hundred or so miles an hour this scraping lean-out, wore away
two thick leather patches, especially positioned, on her racing suit.
'In the States there's a lot of socialising, beer-drinking, after every
race. Here not so much. I guess the more important, the less social-
ising.' Joe.

Both Joe and Alma claimed that the Isle of Man T.T. races were
virtually unknown in the United States. An excellent case for more
publicity there by the A.C.U. What did Joe and Alma do for relax-
ation when they were not racing?
'Well, everything we do is a two-person thing. We go ten pin bowl-
ing and we race long-haired guinea pigs together.'
I must confess that I was too surprised to enquire more deeply into
long-haired guinea pig racing. Now I wonder, are these the beaded,
pot-smoking, long-haired freaks of guinea-pigdom?
Other competitors I had got to know passed out of the paddock on
to the road. On impulse, I rode my motorcycle to Douglas Head.
This is a finger of land jutting out of one end of the bay. From
here you can see all of Douglas and with a turn of the head, the

sea. The air was clear and fresh. Across the bay, now made a metallic silver by the sun, I could see the promenade. Above that, the
Grandstand.

In the clear, cool, morning I could just hear it, a sound like ripp-
ing metal along the dotted line. Even here, far away and high up,
was the noise of the racing two strokes. I rode along the winding
road that clung to the granite cliffs. Stopping to examine some fold-
ed layers of rock on the cliff, a two stroke solo screamed by.
There is no place on the Island where you can get away from
racing over T.T. week.

On Wednesday almost casually in the pits someone mentioned
that they had seen Stan Woods lying on the road at Sulby.
'Stan?'
'Yes, Stan.'
Impossible I thought. Stan is too much of a craftsman to fall off.
'You certain?'
'Yea, stretched out he was.'
As if to confirm this the helicopter chopped its way to the hospital.
I made eqnuiries. He was alive but no-one would comment on his
condition. I went to the A.C.U. office. They fobbed me off with a
bland unconcern which enraged me. I had to know if he was badly
hurt. I felt that in the short time I had got to know him he was my
friend. I wanted to take the grey clerk who ignored all my
questions and shake him until he became a person and not some
self-satisfied bureaucrat.
'It is not my responsibility to comment.'
I walked out trembling with rage.

The next day Stan was discharged from hospital with one arm
out of action and no memory whatsoever of the accident, or the
events leading up to it. He answered my questions abruptly and
then moved off. He was obviously upset that he would not be
racing. For the rest of the time he was very much Banquo, at the
feast of speed. I wondered whether it would be possible by depth

analysis to unblock the memory of the bad accident, or was it a
case of the mind, with some automatic defence mechanism, pre-
venting the destruction of self, through fear or horror at the recall
of the event.

Later that afternoon the times through the speed trap at the
Highlander were published. Some magic few were doing over
150 mph. Findlay was doing over 160 mph. An Australian I spoke
to had come off on his 125cc at Sulby.
'It seized,' said Ross Hedly, with his arm in a sling.
He had a suspected fractured collar-bone.
'Well, that's it I suppose,' I said consolingly.
'No, I think I'll try and ride. I'll see how I feel on the day.'
'What you going to steer with, your feet?' I asked facetiously.
He scowled. 'We'll see.'
In the event he did ride and came thirteenth in the 125cc race and
a few hours later came twenty-seventh in the Formula 750 race.
The pain must have been considerable.

Every practice someone would fall off breaking or grazing body
and machine.
'If it carries on like this I'll tell you one thing, we aren't going to
make any profit.' Helicopter pilot Jim Thirst.
The riders after practice congregated in a large marquee and talked.
They were always conspicuously drunk from excitement.
'Hell at Greeba .... nearly copped it .... ha ha .... one suspension arm had a crack in it, all the way round 'cept for the last
quarter inch of metal. Another lap ....' Incongruously, the young
rider laughed.

Pete Kelly, editor of 'Motor Cycle', was complaining loudly,
'The production Kawasaki we've entered, timed it at the Highlander, he's only doing 132 mph. Bugger must be loafing.'
The factory-rated, top speed of this Kawasaki is 133 mph and the
bike had been entered in aboslutely standard trim.

As Friday approached, with the last practice before the first race on Saturday, everyone was getting more tense.

'*Must* get in another two laps, otherwise we're disqualified,' a grim-faced sidecar entrant.

'I'm not sure about the 750 yet,' said a desperately busy Paul Smart, changing from the 500cc Suzuki to the 750cc. His race in America in the middle of the week had bitten deeply into his practice.

I saw Alan Sansum's wife Christine hurrying from the start line on the Thursday as Alan took off with a roar.

'Don't you stay and watch?'

She paused and looked worriedly at me.

'Oh no, I can't bear to watch him. I get so nervous.'

The ragged edges of a fearful love were visible there, as she hurried on, away from the race. I remembered the riders' faces, grim with concentration controlling their bucking machines, down the straight at Bray Hill and understood, partly, her fear.

On Friday John Williams crashed. There was an angry scene in the pits when his sponsor Gerald Brown confronted the man for whom, as a favour, John was racing one production machine.

'The bike was badly prepared.'

'It was an accident.'

'I've sunk £50,000 into our machines, you've spent what? £500? And badly at that. What have I got now? Bloody nothing. Incompetent . . . .'

The two sponsors were separated, on the point of fighting. Later I went to see John Williams. He looked exactly as always. Neat, his feline face controlled.

'What happened?'

'Came off,' he said.

'How?'

'Well like, I don't want any bad suggestions . . . .'

'Everyone knows.'

'Ah, that's a pity. Yes, me twist grip came off. Bad preparation.

Chapter 7

Now everything's gone.'
'How did it happen?'
'Well, the S-bend at Kerromoor. I was just leaning like over to the right when the twist grip came off in my hand. Doing about a hundred. So I were fighting and struggling to get the grip back on and the wall came up. Well, I scraped that.'
The gouge marks on the concrete I saw later, indicated precisely where this had happened.
'Then I fought it up but I knew that I couldn't win . . . .'
Then in that split second, reflex action, which all top riders have, he decided there was only one possible gap he could aim for, in the blurred death trap of walls, posts and trees. That was some hundred yards away on the other side of the road.
'Well like, something in the back of my mind made me aim the bike and I went for the gap.'
What he aimed for was an opening in between two large beech trees. At his acute angle of approach, the gap between them was minute, about three inches on either side.
'I knew I would have to just clip the low wall in front of them and I did. That flipped me up and through the gap.'
He then skidded along the top of a large hedge of Snowberry which absorbed all his momentum and then deposited him gently on a lawn. His motorcycle bounced off the edge of the low garden wall and gouged and scraped along the road for another sixty or so yards, finally ending up in a ditch. It looked as though some malevolent giant had twisted, torn and finally crunched the machine, in insane anger. John had a broken big toe.
'The ride in the helicopter was quite exciting.'
Would he race again? He looked perplexed.
'Of course. I enjoy it you see. I know I was very lucky, but . . . .
My wife gets a bit worried. She's a dainty sort of woman but she took this well, I suppose she's got to take it. I couldn't pack it up.'
He paused and then added with controlled bitterness.
'I could have won some races this year and now I'm out.'
John went on to explain in detail what a good rider could do 'When the back stepped out.' This was quite clearly child's play compared

to what he had just come through.
When I went back to the scene of John's accident, I was convinced
that only by a miracle was he still alive. Now I am not so sure.
Skill?

A delightful man from Shellsport, Keith Callow, arranged for
me to be taken around the track by Mick Grant.
'He's a good lad, sensible, and he can talk.'
Ray Cunningham, Keith's boss, drove us around, a little bad-temper-
ed to begin with since I was late in arriving. How could I explain
that I was always late for everything?

Mick took me through the circuit explaining the intricacies of
the track on the various bikes. He was riding a 250cc Yamaha, a
350cc Yamaha, a 351cc Yamaha (in the 500cc class, virtually the
same machine as the 350cc but with an eccentric main crankshaft
to give it a marginal extra capacity to comply with regulations), a
750cc Trident, 'Slippery Sam' in the Production race and a 750cc
Kawasaki. He described with precision every major corner, with
candour where he was worried ('I'm not doin' it right here, I can
feel.') and always he came back to the Kawasaki. This was the big
challenge. The other bikes were somehow anthropomorphically
controllable. The Kawasaki alone remained an unknown, its seem-
ingly limitless power awesome.
'On the 250 this is easy, full noise. On the 350 I sympathise with it
a bit. But the Kawasaki . . . . I don't know.'
He recommended that I 'spectate' from Barregarrow, pronounced
Begarra. 'That's where you sort out the real riders. I take it full
'That's where you sort out the real riders. I take it full noise on
them all . . . the Kawasaki gets a bit difficult . . . .' he trailed away
then he brightened. 'Besides spectatin' you get a crackin' good meal
at the farmhouse near there an' cheap too.'
I decided to watch the Senior from there.
Later on, almost abstractedly he remarked, '. . . . that Kawasaki . .'

Unlike Findlay, who disdained landmarks for identification of

Mick and Carol

when to brake, when to start a corner, Mick was a positive British
Museum of items on the track, where he changed gear, riding position (a good rider will brake imperceptibly on occasion, by sitting
up, increasing wind resistance and decreasing speed), where he
accelerated, decelerated, laid the bike over, picked it up and so on.
'At that bench (at Union Mills) I'm two-thirds over on the left,
then for the first bend I cross over on to the white line, stay on it
till *here*, then I pull in to the left hand kerb, then it's hard on,
down one gear, till that drainpipe in the wall *there*, then I throw it
over right and I'm flat out and take the two left handers in one big
swoop and just about clip the kerb.' He smiled at me, 'That's the
classic way of coming around a corner good.'
I learnt that there were sympathetic lines (where the friction between road and tyre is minimised), racing lines (the fastest way
around), classic lines (where the bike looked and felt the best but
not necessarily the best line for the next bend) and wrong lines
(trouble). As we went round Mick unconcernedly pointed out
where he had fallen off.
'Here at Bradden in practice. I coom off in the wet. I skidded
along about thirty yards on my bum   and feet, in a sort of crouch.
As I came to the end of the slide, I just stood up and bowed to
the crowd who clapped, graciously.'
'In last year's Senior I was leading an' there was a patch of oil
which the marshall didn't signal (Ramsay). Well, I hit it and that
was the end of the race for me. Cost me one thousand pounds did
his bit of oversight.'
'At Signpost, in my first T.T. I rammed another rider here. He did
not say a thing. He couldn't, he was out for ten minutes.'
As he remarked, 'Every bend has a tale, some right comical.'
Mick explained how he took the leap at Ballaugh.
'Most take off with their front wheel up in the air and hit the road
with their back wheel. But that's wrong. Look, if you leave off
braking till the last moment, then hit it hard, it puts the nose
down and you've got a second or so. Also, if you land on the back
wheel it thumps hell out of the gearbox and the chain. No I coom
down nose first. Mark you, you do wobble a bit when you first hit

the road.'

During his first race the commentator nearly had hysterics, '. . . . and here's Grant and he's in real trouble at Ballaugh, he's in the air and it looks like a crash landing. Whoops, he's in definite trouble, wobble . . . ah he's away. Lucky.'

No, not lucky, just according to plan.

Mick also told me how to stop quickly.

'You do three things, ninety per cent is front brake (by the way, I hate drum brakes) and a little back, to stop it stepping out and down gears to stop the momentum of the machine fightin' the brakes.'

All of this at once.

Mick occasionally confused the place name of a corner but never the topography or topology of that section.

And then as always back to the Kawasaki. 'It's got enough power to frighten you.'

He complained a little about the new surface on the Verandah. 'Slippy, difficult to know where the limit is.'

As we came to the end of the circuit Mick told me about Governor's Bridge.

'It's the last crack of the whip, you've got to be careful or the road runs away from you.'

In 1972 in the Junior, he took a gamble and did not stop for fuel. He just made it past Governor's when the engine cut. He coasted the last third of a mile to the end and finished third.

'You come out of Governor's in first, through the gears as fast as possible in fifth at the Grandstand, in top on the brow of Bray — and the routine starts all over again.'

Why did *he* race?

'I do it because I get a kick out of it. If I warn't enjoyin it I'd stop. It's my livin' an' if I'm not enjoyin' it I'm not doing it right.'

We all got out of the car and once again I apologised for my tardiness. Ray smiled and drove off. Mick walked to his Transit. What was he going to do now?

'Well, I want to go around the circuit with another rider — want to come along?'

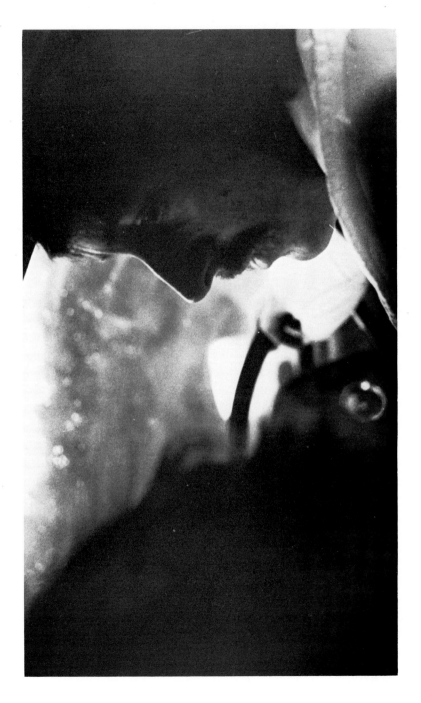

'I've got trubber ere' — Mick Grant

There were some points where Mick was worried and the older rider, Billie McCosh although now slower than Mick, had more experience. Billie was Irish, running slightly to fat, his eyes as blue as the sea.

'Oh I come here and race for the sport ye see. It's the best.'

He had fallen off the previous year and hurt himself badly, yet he was undeterred. We started off the circuit with a joke about the Arabs.

'They don't tell Englishmen, Irishmen and Scotsmen jokes in Ulster, only Arab jokes.'

Then the two riders lapsed into a very private language.

'I'm flat all the way through in third pullin' high.'

'Jettings wrong . . . .'

'Ratios too high here . . . .'

Some time later.

'Do you knock it off here?'

'On the Kawasaki I'm not knockin' it off. I'm just featherin' the fierceness of it. I'll get it flat in the race.'

Then occasionally they would use a linguistic shorthand.

'Here?'

'Down.'

'No!'

'No? . . . I'll try.'

Then they came to Sarah's cottage.

'I'm pathetic here,' said Mick.

Billie looked at him.

'This is verra important ye know 'cause of the next section.'

'I know,' said Mick.

'Show me yer line,' ordered Billie.

Mick took the Transit back and oblivious of the traffic, took it over to the far right hand side and followed a line exactly as he had explained to me in the lap before.

'Well, here I line up on that telegraph pole, then *here* I coom over to the right and then full noise but it's too late.'

He looked at Billie.

They stopped the Transit.

'Go back,' ordered Billie. 'Ye know yer lappin' faster than me but I've watched lots here, and yer doin' it wrong.'
Mick reversed the Transit and Billie said, 'Now I'll show yer.'
He talked Mick through the corner.
Mick was silent until it was completed.
'I can't do it Billie.'
'Listen, those that are flat, are on the line that I'm after tellin' yer. Others are shuttin' off here an' that's a waste of time with the straight after that yer know.'
'Can you accelerate all the way around?' asked Mick.
'On the two-fifty, yes, on the three-fifty, no.'
There was a long silence then Mick shook his head.
'Go on over yon, back to the beginnin' of the corner.'
Mick reversed for the third time and we started again. This time Billie gripped the wheel, the muscles in his forearm showing the effort.
'Now then move her in there, on that black patch *there,* you want to be slightly to the right, then over ter here.' He swung the Transit over. Mick sat in silence. It was plain that Mick had developed an instinctive pattern on this corner and what was happening now was that his intellect was battling with his instinct. Finally he shook his head in exasperation.
'No Billie, I can't do it.'
'Come on 'oot, I'll show yer,' said Billie gently.
They both got out of the van and Billie, pointing and talking softly took Mick inch by inch over the corner. Then they did it again. At the end they stood on the corner all alone, high priests of speed, oblivious and somehow protected from the more lunatic bikers who came roaring around. They got back into the van. Suddenly there was understanding and the tension broke. Mick grinned in delight.
'I see now,' he said. 'In't it amazin' I've kept the same line I had when I first coom 'ere on my old Velocette. An' 'ere's me ridin' a Kawasaki now. Amazin'. Had to unlearn that wun,' he concluded accurately.
Mick started the van and drove on more relaxedly. Billie questioned

him about Barregarrow. Mick described his line.
'An' yer flat?'
'Yes.'
'I don't believe yer.'
Any argument was stopped by Mick.
'Here we are Billie, the ultimate purpose of the trip, Rencullen.'
Billie once again became more authorative, and took the van
through on the line where he could.
'Peel off here and run your shoulder under the hedge.'
'How far under?'
'Till you're touchin' it.'
This at well over 100 mph. Mick looked at Billie.
'Bloody hell, I'm over here you know.'
'I know.'
'John Williams reckons he can get through flat on the three-fifty.
I find that hard to believe.'
'Not as hard to believe as you flat in Barregarrow.'
'I swear Billie,' said Mick in pained surprise. 'It's on the stop.'
Then they reversed and Billie explained the line again.
'Look there's yer line, lift it a wee bit, run down that wall.'
'Aye yes.'
'Keep no further over than the middle of the road. You under-
stand?'
Mick nodded.
'Then it's one big sweep, but if you don't get your shoulder under-
neath, that hedge . . . .'
Then in broad lilt, 'Are yer after understandin' the teery?'
Mick understood the theory.
This corner, since he was so obviously wrong and had changed his
line often, presented Mick no problems in being remembered. Then
there were other corners, more discussion.

I think I can say I have honestly never been more impressed
with two people's dedication, skill and knowledge in my life.
At the Grandstand once again Billie said gravely,
'I'll tell yer an Irish joke. Here's me, Billie McCosh of Ballemeena

lappin' at 100 mph teachin' Mick Grant how to corner, an' he laps at 105 mph.'

Mick laughed.

I asked Billie how old he was.

'Edgin' twenty,' Mick interposed quickly.

'Aye,' lied Billie cheerfully, rubbing his balding head.

I went back to my hotel and thought about the first race soon to be held.

'Some ran out of guts and some ran out of road.'
Observer

There was a palpable tension in Douglas, waiting for the first race to start on Saturday. Sitting in my hotel room I wondered about the riders, how did they feel, what were they doing?

All night long the bikers roared up and down the promenade, engines screaming. They too felt and expressed the tension. Just before dawn there was a brief silence, then the roar started up again. Then another noise joined the cacophony, bellowing, deep and mournful, a fog horn. The bikers appeared and disappeared along the tram lines into the opaque fog, almost in rhythm, to the pulse of the fog horn.

I wondered whether today's race would be cancelled, remembering the one veteran who said, 'We rode through everything, come hail or shine.' In the very early morning, the paddock was eerily quiet. But like soldiers before a mechanical parade, the motorcycles stood waiting, each gleaming, with a cover to keep off the damp, an immaculate line, ending quietly in the mist. There was not a rider to be seen.

I walked around to the press office. Still no riders, but some damp-looking reporters, grumbling dully. The boredom was broken by the arrival of one rider and then a woman.
'Think they'll stick to the programme?'
The rider looked around then towards Snaefell. He shook his head mutely.
'My husband wants to know are they racing this afternoon?'
We all looked at her.
'Tell you what, they should let the sidecar boys race. Doesn't make

Some watched — some waited — some drank

103

much difference to them what the weather's like,' said the solo rider.

'Well, you go and tell them the good news,' said a newsman.

'No, I'll leave that to the A.C.U.'

Ken Shierson, race secretary, appeared out of the fog, looking as worried as ever.

'Are we riding Ken?'

'What's the news Ken?'

He blinked irritably, flicked the ash off his cigarette and pinned a notice to the door.

> *'All races postponed'*

It hung soggily in the fog and drizzle.

'When they going to run then Ken?'

'Ken, I say . . . .'

Ken Shierson gave a half-wave of his hand and disappeared.

'Bloody charming.'

In some mysterious way everyone knew suddenly that there was to be no race. People carried on doing what they were doing, only slower. The pundits now sipped their large scotches instead of gulping them, the sidecar mechanics slowed their frantic but deft assembly of mechanical jig-saws and certainly, some rider, somewhere, made love.

On the next day, Sunday, there being no races, I decided to tour the track myself. I taped a microphone around my neck to record impressions and set off. There were some looks from people as I drove sedately past them, an idiot apparently talking incessantly to himself. But there was something, an atmosphere prevailing, which was even odder. A group of some ten riders passed me at speed, spread out across the road and went into a blind corner. Two of them missed annihilation from an oncoming lorry by a fraction. At the 'Highlander Inn' there was a fearful shouting and waving of hands which made me pull up. A wide-eyed rider, bent over the tank of a big, unbaffled Honda, screamed past me. His mates, pints in hand, jumped up and down and yelled encouragement. Then I noticed that on every bend there were spectators

who were encouraging the bikers into even more suicidal feats.
Riders would roar past, skimming the edge of a brick wall and the
crowd would applaud. The rider would then brake hard, turn
around then repeat the trick, this time striving to go just a little bit
faster and a little bit nearer the wall.

I stopped, bewildered, and I must confess, fearful. I asked a
policeman what it was all about. He tried to look down on me, discovered he could not because I was taller and in retaliation directed some traffic before answering me.
'It's "Mad Sunday". Don't you know?'
'No.'
'Well, they all make like they're Ago or Hailwood.'
I rode cautiously on. But speed being infectious I gradually opened
it out and entered into the spirit of the day. It was then that I
noticed how really bad the average motorcycle rider is. This does
not imply that I am good, simply that most are awful. I followed a
'Triumph' into a corner, he took it too wide, realised his mistake
and braked when he should have been pouring on the power. In
that crystalline moment which preceeds all accidents, the back
wheel drifted gracefully out and away. His footrest kicked out a
rooster-tail of sparks and he cartwheeled off and then rolled along
the road. I pulled up and rode back. He was sitting on a grassy
bank a little stunned, surrounded by his admiring mates.
'I'll tell yer summink when I sore it, I fought, tha's Alf gorne . . .'
'Bloody 'ell, you didn't half ride it.'
'Did I really?'
'You did an' all.'
I rode on not knowing whether to laugh or give him a medal.

On the Veranda, three sidecar combinations passed me. In the
last, a mum with a fat bum, draped herself over the back wheel
and then with total dedication shifted quickly and leant out, over
the family sidecar. She was a little early and the bike wobbled. The
rider glared at her and pursued his two mates. I kept well on the
left, almost off the tarmac and kept my head well tucked in. At

Creg-ny-Baa I stopped and spoke to one of the riders, Doug Lunn, sitting inside his van, watching the riders with a slightly glazed look.

'Have you seen them?' he asked me incredulously. 'They're a bunch of bloody lunatics.'

He was riding one of the big Ducatis.

'Real lunatics.'

That Sunday, two people died and there were 18 serious accidents (the one I witnessed was not classed as serious). I went back to my hotel and waited once again for the first races on Monday, the Junior T.T. (350cc) and the sidecar race.

Most sidecar riders have one frame and two engines. Almost every rider had fitted the combinations with the larger engines in anticipation of the first race on Saturday. There was some apprehension that they would have to put in the smaller engines and then swap over yet again to the big engines. The A.C.U. wisely decided to run the big 750cc combinations on Monday.

'First bloody sensible thing they've ever done, must be a mistake somewhere,' complained one rider unfairly.

Monday was sunny and bright, everything a good race day should be. Even with my myriad of passes I was not quite sure where I could go and what I could do. Could I, for instance, cross the road once a race had started? I decided to start at the Grandstand and work my way around.

The start of the first race was a curious mixture of tension, patriotism and fun, with the first of these moods predominating. Flags of all the nations racing, curled gently in the morning air and the engines screamed and snarled as they warmed up. Then they were ordered to stop and the national anthem boomed out. The riders stood still for a moment and met their hopes and fears. Some more parading of flags by boy scouts scowling intently, then the road was cleared. I glanced up to the race control tower, full, as I knew, of activity.

Inside control, Ken Shierson presided. All over the track
marshalls would be sending in messages by radio and telephone,
messages of crisis or request.
'Yes, I saw you standing in the road before the race,' he said to me
later. 'You were the last off.'
'I was taking a photograph.'
He frowned.
'Don't do it again.'
The control tower is very much the nerve centre of a race. All information comes in here and decisions have to be taken quickly
and correctly. It is like the gallery of a television studio, with one
difference. Mistakes in a television studio can almost always be
corrected and if they cannot, people may be ultimately offended.
At control in a race, a mistake can be fatal. So Ken sweats and
puffs nervously on his cigarette as the messages came in and decisions were made. One macabre point is that the control tower not
only looks out over the straight, but has a perfect view of a grave-
yard, wherein a number of ex-riders are interred.

The Governor-General declared race week open and the 350cc
race began. They started in pairs at ten-second intervals. With a
scream they were away. Mick Grant started near the front and his
eyes tight with concentration looked through me, as I waved to
him.

I discovered that my passes allowed me to walk down the side
of the road, under the supervision of a marshall, who signalled
when I could or could not move. Carefully before the first batch
of riders completed the circuit and after the last rider had gone, I
walked to the bottom of Bray Hill. All the way down, various
radios loudly broadcast information on the progress of the race.
Peter Kneal at the Grandstand handed over to a commentator at
Ballaugh, who hysterically prophesied doom for Mick, landing
apparently disastrously, on his front wheel, as he had carefully
explained. When he did not fall off, he was conveniently forgotten
and the next rider attended to.

'. . . . now there's a good jump, back wheel down and away and . . .'
The crowd, bye and large, were long-haired, leather-jacketed covered with the standard film of grease and good-tempered. One large
Manx policeman presided over the group where I was standing.
'Back there now. Can't stand there. Come on now.'
The crowd moved obediently back. In the distance I could hear
the scream of the two-strokes (all Yamahas, off the shelf racers,
with some modifications but not one single factory sponsored
entrant, by order of the European racing manager, Rod Gould).

Then they came over the brow of Bray. What really surprised
me, even though I had seen it before, was the speed. The road was
empty then suddenly with a scream a rider, crouched over his machine, came by, then another, then another, all close on each
other's heels. The radios gave out the positions, calculated from
corrected time.
'It's Charlie Williams then Rutter, no sorry, Carpenter then Rutter,
then Billie Nelson . . . '
Mick Grant was running sixth, riding the machine John Williams
should have been riding. It had been pointed out to me, that because of a very slight bump on the road, the front wheel of the
bikes would take off. Verbal description bears no resemblance to
the act. The bikes come hammering down the hill, do a slight right
swoop at the bottom, travel uphill then hit the bump. The bikes
scream and lift off the ground, like some monster, rampant horse
and then everything is perfectly still and balanced, as bike and
rider continue along for between 50 and 100 feet at about
130 mph, *on one wheel.* Then the bike's front wheel touches
ground and a few seconds later the riders brake and change down
for Quarter Bridge, an acute right-hander.

It was easy to pick out the really good riders. The 'wheelie'
bothered them not a jot and the machine went into and came out
of it, in a smooth continuous motion. But for some the speed,
bottoming at the end of Bray Hill and the control needed, was too
much. They wobbled and struggled and when they hit the slight

bump they would shut off. This would bring the front wheel down with a thump and then they would accelerate again, losing only a fraction of a second. But it was this fraction which is the difference between a good and an excellent rider.

The circuit is too large to see as a whole and corrected time, read out continuously over the radio, is a necessity. On lap two of the 350cc race the order was Charlie Williams, Tony Rutter, Chas Mortimer and Mick Grant. On the third lap, Williams dropped out with mechanical trouble, then Mortimer retired under similar circumstance. In the end it was Tony Rutter first, ('I was pretty lonely out there with no-one near me') and second, over a minute-and-a-half later came Mick Grant riding safely and unexcitingly. 'I couldn't really get into it,' he said modestly.
A few weeks later he had trouble remembering that he had raced in the Junior T.T. at all, so uneventful was his ride.

After the last rider was in, the marshalls did a quick check of the circuit and then everyone settled down to wait for the 750cc sidecar race, due to begin after lunch.

I wandered down to Quarter Bridge marvelling at the lush green foliage and listening to the bird-songs. Beyond the trees I saw a hot air balloon in a field, 'Guess the height of the Belstaff balloon and win a . . . .' had been the ballyhoo. The height was easy to guess. A dozen or so men were becoming increasingly more desperate, as the wind perversely blew the balloon sideways and down, whenever it arose ever so slightly. The flames, generating the hot air, roared furiously into the empty sky. The men would stop the flame, readjust the huge balloon and turn the flame on again. The wind would slowly topple it sideways, in exactly the opposite direction that the erstwhile ballooners had anticipated. Screams of irritation and rage drifted over the once quiet meadow. After a while the men bowed to the inevitable and slunk away. The balloon lay in the meadow like a giant contraceptive. The cows ambled up and mooed suspiciously over it.

Chapter 8

On the traffic circle at Quarter Bridge, squatting down on his haunches, was a hippie. He had a beautific smile on his face.
'Hi man, how you doing?' I asked.
'A total mind-bender, what a trip.'
A policeman walked up and inspected us. My passes vouchsafed for me. The hippie had problems.
'People are not allowed here.'
'People!'
'Come on now.'
The young man shook his head and his beads clicked delicately.
'See what I mean, man.'
He moved on.

The 750cc sidecar race started. Watching them coming down Bray Hill braking hard for Quarter Bridge I could appreciate how much strength and skill is needed to keep a combination pointing in the right direction. This perhaps accounted for the abstracted air which Joe and Alma Rochelau had had, when I met them prior to the race. They were cocooned by tension and concentration.

On the first lap a sidecar roared up to the circle where I had been speaking to the bearded hippie and the **passenger threw a** battery at a press photographer and a reporter. They were both too stunned to move out of the way and were covered with battery acid. The rider and the passenger roared off again.
'Bloody hell that's ruined my suit.'
'And my camera.'
Another competitor stopped, adjusted something on his motor and then roared off. Alan Sansum seemed to be going well, although he did take the corner a little wide.

I remembered when I first spoke to him at Brands Hatch. He had emerged from under his sidecar, pushed back his curly black hair and looked at me. I repeated my question, was he going to the Isle of Man?
'Yeah. But you know what they've given me, number bloody 25.

Me 25. I ask you . . . . Mind you, I did crash last year, perhaps
that's why.'
I hoped he would not be crashing this year. The Germans as always
zipped by with immaculate precision.

There were hopes that the sidecars would crack the magic
hundred miles-an-hour lap record. On the first lap Steinhausen did
98.18 mph and on the second 87.69 then his Konig engine packed
in. ('I'll tell you Ron, they're no bloody good, O.K. for speedboats,
that's what they're built for . . . . but for here, sidecars ha!' Fred
Lewin.)
One combination retired in front of me and I went to speak to the
driver, Maurice Tombs. He was red in the face and he regarded me
with controlled irritation. Why had he stopped?
'Clutch slipping,' he said abruptly.
Was he disappointed?
He regarded me carefully, went a little redder, then turned away.
Then with a curious gesture of politeness he turned back to me.
'Sorry . . . . it means a lot, you see.'
I nodded sympathetically and left. He looked at his frayed oil-
stained boot and contained his disappointment.

With only three laps to go and a large number of retirements,
the race seemed to draw to an end quicker than usual. I stood on
a wall and took some pictures of the combinations as they came
by. I photographed Fred and Les and some time later, Joe and
Alma. The helicopter chopped its way to Nobles hospital. I wondered who it was.

As always a German won the race. Siggi Schatzau on a BMW. I
walked back to the Grandstand and listened to the winner's interview on Manx radio. There was one slight problem, Siggi did not
speak English. An interpreter was brought in. He too had a problem, he could interpret from German into any language except
English.
The interview started, 'Well Siggi, how does it feel?'

'Wie geht's Siggi? Der Manx Randfunk . . . .'
'Ask him how he feels.'
'Ach zu Siggi und wiefel . . . . '
'So he's fine, how about the race?'
The two Germans chatted animatedly in the background and the interviewer relied more and more on his imagination.
'Well, I can see you've had a good fast race with no problems and it's good to have you here, and I really am pleased to see you win, and I know it was difficult and I hope to see you next year, so thank you sir.'
The last with a little asperity.
Joe and Alma Rocheleau were in the paddock, elated at finishing.
'Wow, what a race, really great.'
'We flipped it you know.'
'Where?' I asked.
'Ramsay Hairpin,' they chorused.
'Someone dropped some oil,' said Alma.
'And we hit it,' said Joe.
'We skidded and flipped right over,' said Alma.
'So?' I asked.
'We turned it over again and carried on riding,' they answered.
Alma's leathers had large holes, where she had worn them through. She looked mournfully at her hands and sighed.
'Gee, I sure do get dishpan hands from holding on to that sidecar.'
I left them to look for Fred and Les. Instead I met Alan. Alan was dejected, as was his sponsor, Rod Quaife.
'We may as well not have come, we've learnt nothing.'
Alan scowled.
'Bloody brake pads started going on the first lap. Get the engine right and what happens, manufacturer gives us the wrong pads. Did the last lap with no brakes. A bit hairy it was . . . . Ah well, better get ready for the next one tomorrow.'

He started stripping the engine out of the combination, helped by his passenger. Fred and Les were nowhere to be seen. I guessed they had broken down. I bumped into Mick Wortley, the man who had explained the intricacies of sidecar combination design to me. He was exuberantly talkative. He had had a great race and come tenth. Next year . . . .

The next day was the International Production machine race for 1,000cc, 500cc and 250cc bikes and the 500cc sidecar race. The Production machines are in theory, standard bikes, that any Tom, Dick or Harry can buy from any dealer, not racing machines. In practice, they are production machines that have been tuned and cosseted by the best mechanics that money and dedication can buy.

I went to bed early, a lot of my new friends would be racing tomorrow. I awoke early and went to the paddock to be met by a smiling Alan Sansum, blipping the 500cc engine which he had just installed.
'Isn't it marvellous Ron, I haven't touched this engine for about six months, I put it in and it starts, first time, sweet as a bird I tell you.'
His son dashed around us on his plastic motorcycle.
I walked over to Fred and Les's Transit. It was deserted.
'Where are they?' I asked a nearby rider.
'Haven't you heard? They lost it yesterday on Sulby. Les is in hospital. Fred's probably visiting her.'
In the quiet morning I recalled Les saying, 'You don't walk away from accidents here.' The helicopter yesterday in the last lap must have been for her.

I went down to the hospital. After some humming and hawing they let me in. Les was in bed trying to conceal her pain. Fred was at the foot of the bed, his hair spikier than usual, smiling in bewildered embarrassment at her. Les had 'bruised kidneys'. How serious was that I asked the doctor?
'Difficult to say just now.'
I went back to the bed.
'It's a bit sore,' said Les softly.

Chapter 8

'It will be O.K.,' said Fred. 'Don't worry.'
Then he looked hard at her and I could feel him tangibly loving
her, assuring her, willing the pain out of her body, into his. His
own body was covered in massive contusions which he never mentioned. All he said later, with old-fashioned simplicity, was that he
'Bathed the real bad parts in salt water — to take the sting out.'
He recounted how the accident happened.
'There were these two havin' a needle match in front of me and I
knew I could take both of them. The tyres were warm, the engine
was sound an' we had no problems. I wasn't chancing my arm you
understand, so on Sulby Bridge one of them swings over and I
think, hello, here's my chance, I'll nip through past both of them.
Then the one sees me and he shuts the door on me. Deliberate.
Came down on my line with his back wheel and hits the front of
my bin. Next thing I knew I hit the side of the wall, crash! Les hit
the wall with her back and got thrown onto the other side of the
road. I couldn't see this. Mind you, this is what they tell me, 'cos I
was doin' funny things with the bike goin' down the road.'
'Who caused the accident?'
Fred looked at me and scowled.
'Ron I can't tell you, but they all know, he's a real nutter.'
A bystander joined in.
'That Mick Wortley.'
'Yea, Mick Wortley.'
Was that why he was so talkative yesterday I wondered?
The bystander added, 'You know Fred when I heard, I said to my-
self, no way would Fred hit the wall 'less he ran out of brakes.'
'Well, it wasn't brakes,' said Fred, then, 'ah well, next year . . . .'

Up at the Grandstand the Production Machine race was about
to start. The riders, all sculpturally athletic in their leathers, strain-
ed forward opposite their machines, in a Le Mans-type start. At the
drop of the flag they sprinted across, started their bikes and roared
off. One Gus Kuhn Norton would not start and the frantic mechanic did something to the transistorized ignition ('The only bloody
thing I can't understand,' he had told me weeks earlier). Another

push by him and the rider and the bike roared to life. The mechanic did a somersault and landed on his bum in front of the Grandstand.

With the big bikes out of the way the 500cc Production race started. I went to the pits to try and get some photographs of the riders refuelling. In the event it was so fast, with so many people pushing and shouting, that I got a fine picture of a blurred gravity filler. I was talking to a woman I had met on practise days when an official came up to her.

'Mrs. Pendlebury?'

'Yes.'

'Your husband has had an accident.'

She blushed a furious red and the mechanic snapped his toolbox shut. Automatically she stopped the stopwatches.

'How is he?'

'On his way to hospital.'

'Well, I suppose it's better to know,' she said with the irrelevance which we all have when suddenly shocked. Pendlebury had broken both legs.

All through the race the helicopter ominously chopped its way from the top of Snaefell to the accidents and then to Nobles hospital. One police chief-inspector confided in me just before the race ended,

'Been a bad one just after the race started.'

'Dead?'

He nodded his head, an imperceptible yes.

'Officially, I don't know.'

'What's his name?'

'Nixon.'

The incongruity of a good man called Nixon dying, while his namesake in America was very much alive and degrading everything he touched, struck me very forcibly.

The reason for Nixon's death is difficult to decide. I have

conflicting statements before me now. One says that he was on the
wrong line around a corner near Glen Helen. ('Undoubtedly the
most dangerous spot is between Ballcraine and Kirk Michael . . . .'
Dr. Pat Cullen.) The other says that he was on the correct line
when his back wheel started drifting, he corrected, hit the kerb
and then hit a wall at high speed. He died of multiple injuries.

After the race in the paddock, the victors in the various classes
were all triumphant. Mick Grant was first in the 1,000cc Production
race on a Triumph named 'Slippery Sam', ' 'Cos it blathers oil out
sometimes.' The absolutely standard 900cc Kawasaki, entered by
Motor Cycle, ridden by Derek Loan came eleventh, the winners of
the 1,000cc, 500cc and 250cc classes posed together, Mick in the
middle, raising his arm encased in plaster and grinning broadly.
'Could hardly see for all the bluddy insects on't screen,' he said.
His perspex windshield was black with squashed, impacted insects.

I went up to Creg-ny-Baa for the 500cc sidecar race in the afternoon. The Germans once again dominated the race. Their immacul-
ately prepared machine roared around the corners providing some
excitement, since their sidecars are on the opposite side to their
British counterparts and they lean out when the British combinations do not and vice-versa.

Alan Sansum came round with his 'sweet as a bird engine', a
500cc Triumph rated in its youth at about 75 brake horse power,
now sounding more like 75 mouse power and sick mice at that.
Alan was scowling furiously.

The winner of the sidecar race was Heinz Luthringshauer on a
BMW and second was George O'Dell, some five minutes after the
leader (a considerable time on the Island) in a sidecar combination
using a Konig ('. . . only good for motorboats Ron . . .') engine.

Luthringshauer later gave an interview to a newsman. While he
was giving it he pulled off one boot, his sock was bloody where

his toes had repeatedly hit the ground. His other boot contained a mass of wood chips. His wooden leg too, had disintegrated under the hammering. The interviewer left speechless.

After the races were over I wandered around the race enclosure. There were books being sold on the T.T., pennants advertising this and that oil, stickers, hats, jackets, everything. In one tent were a large number of oil paintings done in the Soviet-realist-style, of riders past and present, all lantern-jawed and without sin, riding the good ride. The art connoisseurs admired extravagantly. 'I tell you, that Rod Organ (the improbably named artist) is a genius.'

The next day, Wednesday, was the first all solo day, the 250cc Ultralightweight T.T. 'We have to get the sidecars finished first, because they can't afford financially to stay more than a day or two.' A.C.U. official. The day was misty and wet. The 250cc race was scheduled for the morning then postponed. I went to the 'Highlander Inn', had a beer and a pie and waited. All radios were tuned to Manx for the news. '.... postponed until ...' '.... postponed ....' '.... delayed ....' Another beer. I went walking up the road in the drizzle, a policeman called to me. Immediately I checked my passes and conscience. Both were reasonably in order. 'Ah ....' I waited. '.... do you remember me?' I looked at the smart copper. 'Day before yesterday with Findlay.' Recognition dawned. A scruffy, over-talkative man had kept intruding on an interview I was doing with Jack Findlay. 'You?'

Chapter 8

'Yes.'
We chatted while I marvelled on how a uniform metamorphosed
one. On my way back to the Inn a croupier whom I had met the
previous evening in the casino waved to me. He disappeared up a
foothpath with his son and his newly dry-cleaned croupier's suit.
Soon afterwards a car tooted and a man waved, Dr. Pat Cullen.
Truly a small island where everyone knows one another.
'We never have much trouble, everyone knows everyone else and
any trouble-makers have to get on the ferry. Unless the bastards
are very good swimmers.' Manx policeman.

I sat in a car and listened to the radio. The hit of the moment
was
'. . . . and Artie Bell,
Ray Amm, John Surtees and John McIntyre as well,
You can hear their mighty engines, as they run their race to fame
. . . . And their names will live forever,
In the T.T. hall of fame.'
This was sung country-and-western style with the addition of large
blasts of 'the mighty engine's' roar.

Finally it was announced, the race was due to start at four-thirty.
I had another beer and waited.

As four o'clock approached the roads were cleared and by special request the sun appeared, but only at the 'Highlander Inn'.
Elsewhere the track was wet. Waiting for the race to start I could
see a bus travelling on the far horizon to Douglas. Services work
over race week, it's just a question of knowing where to find them.

Then the bikes came, with a high-pitched scream and then an
imperceptible blip as gears were changed, then a scream again.
Changing gear on racing bikes is not like the leisurely shuffle on
an ordinary bike. The riders change gear at about 11,000 rpm, depending on engine characteristics. The co-ordination necessary to
change gear very quickly is close to miraculous. Pull in and release

the clutch, while simultaneously dropping the revs to precisely the correct amount (keeping in peak power band all the time) and flip the gear lever in with the foot, all in a fraction of a second so as not to waste precious revs and speed.

First around was Charlie Williams, closely followed by Mick Grant who was changing gear twice ('The gearin' was all up the spout') once again riding one of John Williams's machines. On lap two, I sat inside a gate and peering through some daffodils watched the riders speed by, at round 130 mph. The order was now Williams, Mortimer then Grant. Up at Creg-ny-Baa, Mick misjudged the corner and had to make a quick decision, hit a wall or slide the bike. With all anchors on he went for the wall.

'Well, I knew that the brakes could bring me down to about ten miles-an-hour before I hit and I might damage the bike if I slid it. So the wall it was.'

The machine seemed in order after the crash so he drove on. Then he smelt burning rubber. He did not know what the matter was but rode 'medium fast' to the pits. Race control knew about the accident seconds after it happened and summoned a scrutineer to Mick's pit stop area. When he stopped to take on fuel, the scrutineers were waiting to check his bike. They checked it in about two minutes and he was off. Bill Rae passed Mick in lap three.

'When I saw that I knew I had better pull finger out, so I did.'

Then he established a lap record. He passed Mortimer at Governors Bridge, about a quarter-of-a-mile from the finish.

'Chas had run out of petrol. Well, we were havin' a dice in the beginnin' and he was trying to psyche me. Laugh, I nearly fell off me bike, you know I felt like stopping and chatting to him about his problems!'

Mortimer pushed his bike across the finish, a minute-and-a-half later. Charlie Williams, Mick Grant and Charlie Mortimer mounted the winners' rostrum, first, second and third. Both Williams and Grant waved their broken arms cheerfully to the crowd, defiantly at the Gods.

Chas Mortimer

On later inspection it was found that Mick Grant had bent his front forks back some two inches on hitting the wall at Creg. The burnt rubber he smelt was his front wheel burning its way through the fibre-glass racing pod. Even so, he broke the lap record. Cool nerve indeed.

That night they gave out the trophies for the races to date, in a large hall on the promenade. Rutter, Grant and Williams, incongruous in suits and ties, waved their winners' trophies above their heads as the crowds roared. The band played 'Deutschland uber alles' for the German winners and there were no incidents.

Mick had advised me to watch a race from Barregarrow (pronounced Begarra).
'That's what sorts the men from the boys, besides you get a crackin' meal at the farmhouse nearby.'
Talking about the Kawasaki here he said,
'I don't really know who's in charge, me or the bike. I have to sympathise with it a bit.'
I was anxious to see just what this corner was really about, so I went there for the 500cc race, the Senior T.T.

It is a wide sweeping corner, a gentle dipping curve to the left with a cottage on its apex, one wall of which juts out, to about a foot from the road. I was certainly not prepared for what I saw. Findlay was first away.

A blue, white and yellow blur came hammering towards the corner and then, in an awful moment, I knew he was going to die. He was going much too fast to control with the precision he needed, the bucking screaming monster, as it plunged towards the wall of the cottage. Then suddenly he was gone, eluding death by a fraction. I must have jumped in fright for the policeman next to me said,
'It's funny, no matter how many you've seen before, you always think they're going to die.'

Chapter 8

The other bikes screamed past with the same heartstopping judgment. Then the weather, never very good, broke. There was wind, rain, drizzle, sleet and some sunshine. A weatherman's dream, they could have said anything and been right. In the cold and rain I thought about Paul Smart.

'I hate the wet, it's better for me to retire than come tenth.'

Jack Findlay, the predicted winner, made two dangerous slithering laps on incorrect tyres and then retired. Mick never made the first lap. He retired at Ballacraine and it was his mechanic who cursed the motorcycle when I spoke to him. Charlie Williams led for halway around, then Phil Carpenter, a relative unknown, but riding like a very hungry man, passed him. Both were riding 350 Yamahas, slightly enlarged in capacity to qualify them for the 500cc race.

'You see, it's not a question of power. We've already got more power than we can usefully use, suspension, roadholding is the thing.' Jack Findlay.

In the wet this was doubly so. The weather on the mountain was atrocious. One rider was blown off his bike at the aptly named 'Windy Corner'. The riders passed and repassed Barregarrow, kicking up rooster tails of water, doing impossible speeds under impossible conditions. Charlie Williams, blond and bespectacled, found his glasses misting up.

'It was silly to try and go faster. I couldn't see.'

Phil Carpenter won and attributed it to the rain.

'Couldn't stand riding in other people's spray so I passed them.'

Carpenter first, Williams second. Billie McCosh riding a workmanlike race came fourteenth and won £50.

'He's sponsored by the people of Ballymena who buy his cars.'

Mick Grant on Billie's source of income.

When the cold miserable race was over I went for the 'cracking good meal' at the farmhouse. After lunch the sky spitefully cleared and the sun came out. I learned that some of the riders were, at the end of the race, so cold that they had to be lifted off their

At the end of this one some of the riders were literally frozen stiff

motorcycles. It must have warmed the old timers' hearts.

I planned what I would do on the last day. This was the big race, the 'Formula 750'. Norton had bet everything on it, sponsorship, honour, glory and they were confident. Suzuki had a specially designed bike, there was Mick's Kawasaki and a host of others. The lap record would go. This was to be the most exciting race of the T.T. period. Preceeding it, almost anti-climatically, was the race for 125cc bikes. I decided to sit this one out and observe the medical services.

The morning was perfect, sunny and warm. One rider fell off his bike in the 125cc race and was brought into the hospital. His friends and wife waited anxiously outside. Then he emerged, broken collar bone strapped up, his leathers around his waist. He hugged his wife consolingly and she gave a nervous grin. There were no other accidents. I went up to Creg-ny-Baa for the 750 race.

Tony Jeffries, a young ex-rider, crippled in a crash, started them off from his wheel chair. Soon after the race started, the weather broke and ruined everything. The 750cc race-bred monsters, straining under too much power, baulked when held in. They spluttered, oiled up and refused to remain tractable.
'I was getting wheel-spin every time I changed gear in the wet. Yer see me arm was in plaster. No delicate control, no wrist movement. It was very hairy, then the plugs oiled up 'cos I didn't open it out.' A disconsolate Mick Grant, explaining just what it means to have your throttle hand in plaster, riding a very hot Kawasaki on a wet track. Mick stopped to change his oiled up plugs and replacing them put him back twelve minutes, into seventeenth place.

All hopes of breaking Hailwood's lap record disappeared on the wet roads. The lap speeds to begin with were only marginally faster than the 250cc bikes. This was not surprising as some parts of the course were wet and some dry, the most difficult of all conditions. Surprise of the race was Percy Tait riding a 750 Triumph. A veteran of many races he was cheered all around the circuit on his last lap. He came fourth. One, two, three, were Chas Mortimer (350 Yamaha), Charlie Williams (ditto) and Tony Rutter (ditto). The big monsters had been roundly and soundly beaten.

There were no serious casualties which was something of a miracle, given the conditions of the track and as I drove to the Grandstand I suddenly felt pleased. None of my new-found friends had been injured. At the Grandstand with almost indecent haste the marquees were coming down and the seagulls swooped and dived in the empty paddock. After all the tension, excitement and then the let down of the last race, I wanted something more, another race. I spoke to an oil company representative about the failure of the big stars to make a showing in both the 500cc and the 750cc races. 'Some ran out of guts and some ran out of road,' he said, and I agreed with him. But then I thought that after all I was merely an observer, not a participant and it ill became me to say or think, '*You* lacked courage,' for surely *I* would have done the same. But undeniably, some riders in the last two races, were lacking something, but not dishonourably. They merely became human, not gods.

Chapter 9

'It's not only a race . . . .'
Peter Strong, 'Motor Cycle News'

I went back to the T.T. races a year later (1975) to write this final chapter. Also after the work and interviews I did in the previous year (1974) to relax and enjoy the races.

Very little had changed, the argument as to whether to demote the races from world championship status still continued, although it now looks as if 1976 will be the last year that the races count towards championship status. The F.I.M. sent over an observer and unfortunately, two more riders were killed in virtually the same spot while he was there. This did not deter one Manx Radio commentator (Tony Robb I think) from making an impassioned plea to him on air, just before the start of the Senior.
'. . . . just tink of all de pleasure we gets . . .' with the Irish accent laying on the agony. He should, of course, have been describing the conditions of the track at Ballacraine.
The editors of the two main motor cycle publications were unanimous about what the loss of championship status would do.
'Best thing in the world to happen to the T.T.' Pete Kelly, 'Motor Cycle'.
'It's not only a race, it's also a social event, championship status is a lot of rubbish.' Peter Strong, 'Motor Cycle News'.

What does need to happen, is that if the race is to compete with Daytona, the other motorcycle classic (which has no international status), it will need a lot more money to attract the top stars. One thing is noticeable, spectators and riders go to circuit racing for a day or at most two days. On the island people come for two weeks, one week's practise, one week's racing. A whole different spirit is engendered, more friendly, people meet old friends and the veterans relive the times when the race 'really was a race'. On top of this the Isle of Man is undeniably beautiful.

Between races I went to Port Erin and Peel and knew that in looking on the fishing smacks in the harbour and shivering at the sea smells, I was imbibing something that was timeless, enduring and magnificent.

If the atmosphere and the race had not changed, some of the riders had. Peter Williams, ex-Norton rider, had damaged himself badly in a crash on a circuit. He spoke to me thoughtfully and at length about the T.T. races. He was definitely still an afficianado, but maintained that the prize and/or start money would have to go up if the race was not to become yet another British anachronism, ignored by the rest of the racing world. People came up and he signed his name on whatever was available and he joked about the transcience of fame.
'Used to be they'd refer to Tony Rutter as Peter Williams' brother-in-law, now they refer to Peter Williams as Tony Rutter's brother-in-law.'
A wry smile.

Barregarrow was for him always the most terrifying place on the track and is so for most riders, yet strangely enough no accidents happen there.
'My sister, Andrea, first watched me race on the Island from Barregarrow and when I went past she burst into tears. Never been back there since.'
I left him with his memories of the track, his one arm shrunken and immobile. I doubt whether he will ever race again.

Paul Smart was absent; he had been in a bad accident on his works Suzuki. The accident had taken place on a circuit. He blamed the bike and his remarks about it were, as always, succinct.
'About time they designed a proper bike and stopped patching this bloody one up.'

Barregarrow - still the most exciting corner

It was at Jurby airfield that I saw most of the other riders. First-
ly the airfield. I am fascinated by old and derelict buildings and
since Jurby airfield, virtually unused since the war, is liberally
sprinkled with disused hangars and control towers, it is very much
to my taste. 'All pilots to report to control on landing,' proclaimed
a battered notice, hanging drunkenly from a door.

From the top of the control tower, in the distance, you can see
and hear the motorcycles as they streak along the runway, accelera-
ting, breaking, turning and repeating the process once again. In the
tall grass surrounding the runways a myriad of birds flew and returned on mysterious errands, ignoring the rush and racket of the
bikes. The purpose of Jurby, for riders and mechanics, is to test
the motors generally and since Jurby is at sea level, corresponding
to the Selby straight, to get the carburation right. So the bikes
would scream up and down, the plugs would be unscrewed rapidly,
scrutinised for tell-tale signs of incorrect mixture and then the jets
adjusted accordingly.
'Down two I think.'
'O.K.'
And off again.

I climbed down from the disused control tower and joined the
riders. Jack Findlay was there; he too had been dropped by Suzuki
and was now riding for Norton in the International Open Classic.
He had just flown in from another race on the Continent and was
changing into his leathers. His face crinkled into a grin when he
recognised me and then he apologised for not replying to a letter I
had written to him.
'Bloody Italian postal service . . . . world's worst . . . . must go.'
The Norton claimed his attention.

Jack was getting used to his bike while on the other Dave
Croxford was practising refuelling. In a precisely choreographed,
high-speed ballet, Croxford would roar to a stop, petrol cap off,
fuel nozzle in, while Croxford would lean forward blindly and

grasp a wet rag placed precisely in the mechanic's pocket. Quick
wipe of visor, drop rag, snap and clatter of tank and nozzle and a
away in a roar. Frank Perris, team manager, clicked his stop watch.
Jack Findlay rode up and down frowning. It all looked very impressive.

On the day of the race both bikes completed just over a mile
and then ground to a halt. As one ex-Norton mechanic explained,
when I asked him what he had done with the bikes he had worked
on last year,
'Well, I dug a very deep hole, then I pushed them in, then I covered it up.'

In distinct contrast to this was the production bike 'Slippery
Sam', a Triumph Trident. 'Sam' completed and *won* the new ten-
lap producton race (377 miles long) 'without ever missing a beat',
said Percy Tait, one of the winning co-riders. There was some speculation as to who was the oldest, Tait or 'Slippery Sam'. But
while the jokes and the happy aura of winning surrounded Tait and
co-rider Croxford, I remembered one old Meridan worker explaining why he was in favour of making Triumph motorcycles, when
everyone was trying to close them down.
'They're quite simply the best motorcycles in the world.' Then he
looked at his hands. So here's to 'Slippery', eight Isle of Man wins,
perhaps the old man is right.

At Jurby I also bumped into Charlie Williams and his mechanic.
He was tuning one of his Yamahas for the Junior T.T. To me he
has always been one of nature's gentlemen, cheerful, kind and
helpful. Moving with the grace of the natural athlete he is, he circled his bike inspecting it, then he saw me and we chatted a while.
His mechanic signalled him and with a smile he was off with a high-
pitched scream of the two-stroke.

Some days later his bike seized as he took off at Ballaugh. For a
microsecond, when he landed, it was touch and go whether he was

going to slam violently into one of the ever-present stone walls. By dint of sheer skill he wrestled his bike into a straight line and stopped it. 'Bit close,' he smiled gently when I asked him about it later.

Mick Grant also appeared at Jurby to tune his vast multitude of Kawasakis. This year they had bred yet another monster, a water-cooled 750. If last year's Kawasaki was scaring, this one was positively terrifying. It occupied all of Mick's waking hours (and I suspect a great deal of his sleeping ones as well). The great green brute, even in static silence, emanated a vast field, of malevolent force and power.
'Trubble is, I just have to touch that throttle like this', a delicate flick, 'and I get wheel spin. Any speed, any gear, any tyre.'

Mick won the 500cc Senior race, riding superbly and stylishly. In the international classic the big Kawasaki was clearly the bike to watch. From a standing start all eyes and clocks were on them. The weather was ideal and the circuit dry, unlike last year. Due to the logistics of the race (standing start, pit stops for fuel etc.) the only crack Mick would have at Hailwood's long-standing record would be at laps two, five and six, if he had enough fuel for three laps, which was itself not known.

Interestingly enough Mike 'The Bike' Hailwood was at the T.T., his one leg still badly damaged from a crash he sustained in a racing car. He did a lap of honour piloted by his old rival, Geoff Duke, on some super-duper monster, fresh from Japan. So Hailwood too was watching Grant. Mick looked like a winner all the way and then on lap two an almost hysterical announcer screamed out that the magical time, the absolute lap record, set by Hailwood in 1967, had been beaten by Mick Grant. For a moment a number of us knew that the equally magical 110 mph lap was within Mick's grasp.

And then nothing — Mick disappeared from the leader board. Something had gone wrong with his chain adjuster, with it went a lot of hopes and money. But then that's the island, it really does

John Williams on his big win

stress and test everything mechanical, very near to and sometimes past, destruction. Hailwood's record still stands in the 500cc class. Perhaps Grant, or Williams (John), or Williams (Charlie), will bust that next year, or next, or next.

With Mick out of the big international race, John Williams riding a 350 Yamaha went on to collect first place. He climbed up the winner's rostrum, looked at the position reserved for the winner, stepped on to it very slowly and then quite deliberatly stamped his foot on it for all to see. 'This is mine' he was saying. He clenched his fists and raised his arms. The crowd went wild. There was about him all the aura of a man who had triumphed where he once failed. I was happy for him.

The International Open Classic was the last race of the T.T. week and once again the seagulls wheeled and cried and people fed them, despite a Manx radio warning that 'the most dangerous thing you can do is to feed the seagulls'. There is an element of the truth in this statement surprisingly enough for at very high speed a sea-gull becomes not a bird but a projectile when hit by a bike.

Once again a curious stillness settled with almost indecent haste over the pit area. I wandered down from the Grandstand remembering a rider I had seen at Bray, about half-an-hour earlier. He had gone into a wheelie and then came down again, hard and very fast. Immediately his bike started weaving. Here I learnt what the phrase 'tank slapper' meant. The front wheel went into a high speed oscillation, banging the handlebars on the tank. The rider did not decelerate, but actually *accelerated* his way out of a situation, which I thought was uncontrollable and potentially fatal. It was while I was reliving this moment, when every spectator including marshalls were certain they were going to see something rather nasty happen, that I saw Neil Tuxworth. He was sitting on the lawn, with his girl-friend, his bike in the background. He had just come fourth in the 'Open'. What was he doing, drinking champagne, eating caviar? Neither, actually, he was slowly and silently licking an ice cream.

I left him and the race and the Island and caught the ferry home. But like the year before, for weeks after the race I could not get it out of my mind I walked around like some numb-struck adolescent, repeating to myself certain phrases of the riders and having them re-echo in my mind. So now I set them down, for the music to come alive for you as well.

> 'Coming into this tunnel of woods
> I love the smell,
> And then the sun hits you.
> But I'm pathetic here,
> I have to feather the fierceness of it.
> Can you help me?
> And here, this is super,
> You crank it over
> And all you can see is sky
> And I'm flat, all the way
> In third and pulling high.
> Then here, the road runs away
> If you leave it too late.
> It's the last crack of the whip
> Before the Grandstand . . . . .
> On the brow of Bray, in top,
> The routine starts —
> All over again.'

Chapter 10

Technical Data

250cc Honda, Yamaha, Suzuki etc.	Juice
350cc Yamahas etc.	More juice
500cc Honda, Suzuki, Yamaha etc.	Lots more juice
750cc Big S, Big K, TZ Yam	Jesus Christ!